ARE YOU READY YET?

Preparing For a New Relationship

JOHN GORDON

ILLUSTRATED BY RAY JELLIFFE

PICCADILLY PRESS · LONDON

I dedicate this book to Bunty, to whom I am grateful for twenty-one years of wonderful partnership and to Susi, my new partner who has given me great loving support and help in writing this book.

Phototypeset by First Impressions, Lingfield, Surrey
Printed and bound by Biddles, Guildford, Surrey for the publishers
Piccadilly Press Ltd.,
5 Castle Road, London NW1 8PR

A catalogue record for this book is available from the British Library

ISBN 1-85340-104-8 (trade paperback)
ISBN 1-85340-198-6 (hardback)

John Gordon is British and lives in Sussex. He is separated after twenty-one years of marriage, and he has two children. He is now enjoying a new relationship. In addition to founding and running his own travel business, he has built up an excellent reputation in relationship counselling and personal growth.

Ray Jelliffe is British and lives in Berkshire with his wife. Now retired, but working harder than ever, he illustrates greeting cards and books. The books illustrated for Piccadilly Press include *Europe United* and *A Riot of Writers*. In his previous life he was the creative director of a large advertising firm.

INTRODUCTION

Chapter One
THE BASIC TOOLS FOR DISCOVERY

Chapter Two
LEARNING ABOUT YOURSELF

Chapter Three

IT IS AS IT IS

Chapter Four

MOVING ON

Chapter Five
CHANGE

INTRODUCTION

I have written this book for all of you who want real love
in your lives, who want to learn from your past experience
of a long-term partnership, who do want to make your
lives more creative, and to be more 'attractive' in all kinds
of ways. It is for those of you who do want to find a way
to create a new partner in your life, someone who will
love and accept you for your true self.

My aim is to help you to be more in touch with your
own needs, to learn from and release your personal
relationship history, to identify any blocks to your
happiness, so that you can begin to create a life in which
you can express and receive love safely.

In writing this book I have drawn on my own
experience, both in my personal life and while working
professionally with individuals and groups. I invite you to
share with me the processes and techniques I have
developed, which have proved effective. You will also
read some personal accounts of those who have
successfully applied these practices to their lives.

This book is easy to read, the techniques are simple to
follow, and powerful. It is designed to allow you to work
through it step by step or to concentrate on some of the
sections that really appeal to you. However you use this
book the ideas and practices in it will help you to feel
more in charge of your life. You will be able to make
positive and informed decisions about your readiness for
relationship and then move on to create a loving
partnership in your life.

This is a 'how to' book. Mostly it's a 'read it', 'just do it',
'feel it', 'think it', 'let it all hang out', soothing, healing
book - it is a book to have fun with.

Chapter One

THE BASIC TOOLS FOR DISCOVERY

A. CELEBRATING OUR DIFFERENCES

We all have different ways of 'being' in this world, and it is good to celebrate the fact that we are all different, and respect that. Relationships might be easier if we were all the same, but then they would not be as interesting.

Throughout this book you will be offered various ways of checking the reactions inside yourself. This is a way of getting to know yourself better and to be more confident in your choices.

You can find out how you communicate by asking yourself a series of questions:

- What do you feel about this?
- What do you think about this?
- How does that look to you? Do you get the picture?
- How does that sound to you?
- How does that touch you?

If I ask you how you feel about some things and you really need to ask yourself, "What do I think?" then you can change the question to suit your own way of being.

B. THINKERS AND FEELERS

In the past and even today, boys are taught to be 'thinkers' and girls 'feelers'. It is often possible to hear this in the language that they use. There is no reason why this should be so and it would be good to change it. If you were brought up in this way, switch them around and 'see' what you 'think' you 'feel'. Does that 'sound' like it 'touches' you somewhere?

C. Visual Ideas - Picturing

What is happening is that you are seeing the picture on the outside, on the screen, and creating another picture on the inside, on your internal screen with yourself on it. You know those films with passionate love scenes? Do you imagine yourself doing the same thing, and for that moment having a beautiful body? Do you experience the passion, the excitement, the lust? We are always creating pictures in our mind and here is a simple test:

Close your eyes and describe each part of the house that you live in, upstairs, downstairs and the garden if you have one. You will notice that your eyes are physically following a picture of your house that you have created in your mind. This is called 'visualisation' and it is a powerful tool in creating for you the kind of life you would like to have and attracting the people you would like to have in it.

1. Create a picture in your mind of a beautiful place and include an imaginary ideal partner.

2. Put yourself in the picture.

3. Imagine this is actually true and note how you are feeling.

4. Your mind now knows what to do, and you will begin to make choices that will lead you to attract what you want into your life.

Picture Plus Feeling = Desired Result

D.   MAKE IT SIMPLE

My first experience of working with young people was for three months, with a group of highly talented school drop-outs, aged fourteen and fifteen. We had a wonderful time and they opened their hearts willingly as they travelled deeper into themselves and found more of their self-worth. They were a great audience to my ideas on raising self-esteem and effective living. I loved them all, and they taught me one of the most important lessons of my life.

At various times during our daily sessions, one of the group, Alethea, would stop me and say... "John, make it simple." I would stop and do my best to repeat what I had just said using half the number of words. She would then, at a later stage, say it again, and I would halve the words again. I noticed that each time I halved the number of words I used, the point I was making became clearer and more powerful.

I therefore pass this message on to you. If your life is complicated - make it simple. Begin to let go of as much as you can that makes it complicated.

1. Where have you needlessly relied on others for direction? Whom have you listened to? Have you sought advice from just anyone you happened to be talking to? Do you think it would help you to talk to someone with experience, maybe a counsellor?

2. What are the things you say to yourself that build up or tear down your self-image? How do you feel when you put yourself down? How do you feel when you don't? How often do you speak well of yourself?

3. Do you have strong beliefs about yourself that were formed by someone else's opinion of you? Do you still want to keep them?

   Think of a wonderful and positive experience you have had and then picture yourself doing it now. Do you feel good?

   Practice picturing in your mind something you really want to happen. Do you enjoy the feeling of anticipation this brings you?

By letting go of all that does not feel good in your life and keeping your mind centred on what does, you can make your life simpler and clearer.

E. SHARING FEELINGS AND EXPERIENCES

There is a belief that women find it easier than men to express their feelings, especially to each other, and because it is a widely held belief, it still mostly remains true. Men have been encouraged to keep their feelings to themselves, to keep a 'stiff upper lip'. Here is a chance of a light break... Try talking right now with your upper lip held stiff... Did you find that first of all you sounded like you had no teeth and secondly you could not put any expression into your voice... Interesting?

This belief and indeed expectation causes the pattern to go on repeating itself, until someone decides to change it. There are self-help groups of various kinds, many of which are about self-improvement, to enhance the quality of life, and to break free from limiting patterns. One of the more recent developments for men is 'men's groups', which have provided the opportunity for groups of men to get together and share deep and intimate feelings, to be able to talk out their frustrations and even to cry in a safe, supportive atmosphere.

It is said that "the best thing that has happened for women is men's groups". The opportunity to express their darker, angry and more vulnerable self to another man, has changed the way that some men are able to relate to women and each other. Men discovered that they were able to express strong loving feelings towards other men, without the perennial male fear of being labelled homosexual. This feels like a great step forward, and will enable men and women to have a more loving relationship with each other. Any opportunity to feel safe, expressing feelings and having them respected is good. It is a lot of energy in a group, and it's great fun, especially if it is mixed.

F. RELAXATION

There are many reasons for the ending of a partnership. There will always be a lot of stress. If the ending was abrupt there is likely to be an experience of shock.
If the partnership dragged on for some time there would inevitably be arguments and emotional trauma. The body becomes stressed, and it can take a long time to recover.
I have worked with many people who have experienced this kind of shock and it may be years later that their body reacts with physical symptoms.

The body loves to take in deep breaths and plenty of oxygen.

More tension leads to shallower breathing
Which means less oxygen in the blood-stream
And therefore less to the brain
The thinking then becomes confused
Confusion leads to self-doubt
Which leads to defence mechanisms and the building of 'walls'.

How can this stress be relieved?
Exercise is one way and can be very positive. It can be dangerous if the stress remains and is not released, leading to accidents and overworking of the internal organs, especially the heart.

6

Relaxation is another way and can be practised anywhere - in your bedroom, on the loo, in a train, on a bus, anywhere. I find that when I am relaxed, everything works well, and with no conscious effort, my breathing improves. I am able to be more honestly in touch with more truth about myself, and *less willing to let my fears run my life.*

When you are relaxed you feel good and when you feel good, others around you catch the atmosphere and then surprising things happen. Deals are made, decisions are reached, there is a greater sense of acceptance and loving and more freedom to experience more of each other. The whole world looks safer and more friendly.

THE STRESSBUSTER:

- Loosen any tight clothing... find a comfortable and relaxed position.
- Take a deep breath... hold it for a while... Now let go... Take another deep breath... hold it for a while... This time, when you let go, make the sound Haaaaaahhh. Now breathe normally for a few moments, and concentrate on nothing else except your own breath. Next inhalation tell yourself, "I am easily" and on the exhalation tell yourself "relaxed"... (Inhale) "I am easily" (Exhale) "relaxed".
- Repeat this a few times. When you say the word "relaxed" to yourself, let your body slowly sink deeper and deeper into the chair or bed. During the day you spend a lot of energy fighting the force of gravity. Now for a few moments let that force take you over completely. Now... repeat each of these phrases to yourself. "I let every muscle, every fibre, every cell in my body, be pulled down and down... farther and farther down... I feel my body slowing down... and my mind slowing down. There is no rush... no hurry. There is nowhere I have to go...

nothing I have to do." Tensions and frustrations are gradually seeping out of your system. Every time you breathe in imagine you are breathing in a wonderful glow of relaxation, and every time you breathe out, imagine that you are breathing out all your tensions, tiredness and frustrations. A feeling of peace washes over you and through you. It is so calm, so quiet... so silent. Say... "I give myself permission to be... calm... quiet... silent. The silence feels warm and comfortable and healing... deeply healing... I feel at ease... and at peace... at peace with myself and all that is around me... at peace with the whole world."

G. SAFE PLACE

In various ways I offer you the idea of feeling safe. You will notice that I use the word safe often. Most of the time we exist in what could be called a 'safety zone', a place where we can keep within limits. The habits of a lifetime can restrict our way of being. Our fears limit the way we are able to be with others, and we gather around us a set of friends to ensure that we do not have to move out of this space. Have you noticed that all your friends like you?! Being in this 'safety zone', being the way you are and meeting the same kind of people is fine, but this may limit your life. If you do not meet any new people you may become somewhat frustrated and tighten that circle of 'barbed wire' even more, in order to feel safer. Is this your experience? Do you find yourself nervous at parties, uncomfortable with strangers, self-conscious in unfamiliar situations? What else?

In order to experience more of life and more of yourself it helps to expand your safety limits and there are many ways of accomplishing this.

1. You can wear different clothes to the ones you are used to or feel comfortable in.
2. You can risk being a little more assertive, where you have been lacking in self-confidence. This nearly always applies to how you relate to others.
3. You can discard old habits, and although this may well feel like too much, bring up old fears. Creating safety helps you to walk through these fears and emerge stronger and with a greater sense of self-worth.

There is a fine lady, who comes to see me regularly for counselling and therapy, and on each visit she has new problems. I asked her one time, what would happen if she had no more problems. She replied, "Well, I couldn't come and see you any more." The fear of change and loss is real and brings up many thoughts of not being able to cope in a new situation or a new relationship.

Feeling safe means that you can move forward. It only takes a little while to get used to new conditions. I know many who have 'jumped' and landed fairly and squarely on their own two feet, nourished totally by the experience, into great new relationships.

Chapter Two

LEARNING ABOUT YOURSELF

A. RELEASE AND LET GO

There is an old sixties song, which goes 'Please release me, let me go, for I don't love you any more'. If you have been in a long-term relationship, there will be so much that you have shared with your partner. There will be many bonds that you created which were the basis for your partnership. These 'bonds' can be very strong and even after the partnership is long over, they can still be there and form a resistance to creating new relationships.

   We also have patterns from childhood that we learnt from the example of our parents. You may notice that you have in some way re-created the same ones as them. Have you done what they did?

   Releasing and letting go of these bonds from the past allows you the freedom to attract a new partner who is nothing like your father or mother or brother or sister, or even your ex-partner, who will be a totally 'new' experience for you. By absorbing what you want from this book and by participating in some of the suggested exercises you will find the process of letting go and releasing becomes both easier and more rewarding.

B. YOUR RELATIONSHIP WITH YOUR REAL-SELF

Psychologists tell us that most of our patterns, habits and ways of reacting are created in the first three years of our lives, and after that we just go on repeating the same kind of patterns and the only difference is the context in which they happen. There is a strong tendency for adults to react to life situations and especially relationships, in the same ways that they learnt as children, and to copy their parents' attitudes and ways. Often you hear the cry of women who say "I hope I don't get to be like my mother." Well you've probably had a great head start. You were well into it by the time you were three!

Babies have an innocence which makes them powerful beings. They have an innate knowledge that they will get what they want and that their needs will be met. At an early age their needs are simple and essential for life support: warmth, food, sleep and love. By the time babies are born they are already used to having their needs met inside the mother's womb, and upon arrival in the world, they consider themselves entitled to receive nourishment on all levels, and there is no other thought in their minds than that they are beautiful, totally deserving, always right and completely safe. Can you imagine how it would be if we all retained these beliefs? Can you imagine how easy and totally rewarding our relationships would be? If the environment into which the baby is born is not loving and caring, a different kind of knowing is imposed on its original innocence. Life becomes more complicated. With a sense of unsureness the baby's demands become greater, beginning to ask for more than it needs, just to be reassured. The way of demanding becomes stronger, and it learns how to manipulate.

C. DISCOVER YOUR REAL-SELF

This can be the learning that we take into our adult lives, and into our relationships. We need to unlearn all these ways, discover again our innocence, combine it with the wisdom of our experience and the ability to be patient. Babies love to improve the quality of their lives, to make life more fun, safer, more comfortable, more special and to

11

achieve their every desire. If they have a picture in their mind of something they want, they will not rest until they get it.

This innocence, this knowing and trusting does not go away. It is our 'Real-Self', the real you that believes that life is simple and all your needs are met all the time.

This real you may be the one that you are searching for, when you are seeking for some identity, some answer to the question "Who am I?"

D. TRUST YOUR REAL-SELF

You can ask your Real-Self for guidance on anything. It will never let you down and will always give you the best and clearest answer. Sometimes this is called your 'True-Self', 'Higher Self' or even 'intuition' or 'a hunch'. Your Real-Self knows exactly what you need at any given moment and also knows the best way you are able to meet this need. It is not affected by learned habits, fears, guilt or negative reasoning.

When you ask yourself what to do in a situation, there is always a 'first thought' and then there is a second. The second thought is weighed down by the past, fearful of the future and determined not to change. The first is inspirational and your Real-Self.

For much of your life you have tried to be something for someone else, either what they wanted you to be or in a more rebellious mood what they do not want you to be. You may have been the 'good boy' or the 'good girl' or the 'naughty one', that gets away with everything. You may have been the youngest or the eldest, the tall or thin, or strong or weak or 'brainy' or good-looking or kind or lazy or 'not good enough' one. *"Mary can do better, with a little more effort." "John needs to pull his socks up to keep up with the rest." "David sails through life so easily. He is very lucky." "Nicola is beautiful, she will stun all the boys."* All these messages from childhood colour the way we are in adulthood, trying very hard to act out or to rebel against what we were told about ourselves.

In relationship, your programmed self meets another programmed self and then we wonder why we don't feel real together and can't get any further in our partnership.

Being your Real-Self is letting go of preconceptions of who and what you are and finding more of the real you to explore, know and love.

E. RECOGNISE YOUR REAL-SELF

There is no race to get anywhere, no marks out of ten, no success or failure, no wrong turnings, just where you are at this moment... I honour and trust that where you are is the right place to be right now and that it takes as long as it takes, no longer or shorter.

13

You are unique, nobody in this world is like you, no-one has fingerprints like you, no-one thinks like you, talks the same way as you do. You are very special and have a unique contribution to make in this world.

I ask you to gradually develop an affection for yourself to value all your qualities and to decide when you want to let them be useful in the world you live in, and when you want to share them with a new partner.

You are not what your previous partner or your parents or teachers or brothers or sisters or friends or bosses say you are. You are not even your job or your house or your car or your status. As you let go of these old concepts of yourself you become closer to the Real-Self and then you can meet someone who loves this new Real you.

Be sure to get to know your Real-Self better, just so that you will be able to recognise your real partner, when you are introduced.

You are your Real-Self and a deeper relationship with this Real-Self will enable you to make choices as to when you are ready for a new 'RELATIONSHIP' with a new partner.

F. POWER

This word has many different effects. Pause for a moment, say the word "POWER" out loud and notice your own reaction to the word. Now say "I AM POWERFUL"... How was that?

The word derives from the old French verb 'poeir', which means 'to be able'.

Now repeat this, and notice if your energy changes:

> *I love to be powerfully loving.*
> *I love to be powerfully loved.*
> *I love to be powerful.*

14

Respect all your thoughts and feelings without judgement.
Another way of expressing these feelings would be to say:

> *I love to be able to be loving.*
> *I love to be able to be loved.*
> *I love to be able.*

Check for yourself if there is a difference and allow
yourself to make the connection between power and
ability.

At this point we can also consider the world *disabled*,
putting it in a physical and mental context. Some who
have a 'disability', are able to overcome it and become
powerful people, but many are disempowered and find
themelves dependent on others. This certainly happens in
relationships and so many are based on one partner
compensating for the other's inabilities. This is fine for a
while, and then it leads to resentment, jealousy and anger
at the feeling of dependence that has been generated.
Being independent does not mean being alone. It means
having all that you need in yourself at any moment, and
then being able to share this with like-minded friends,
lovers or partners.

G. POWER WORDS

Words that *enable*.

Being ready for a new relationship is about feeling good
all over and wanting to share it with another person. This
is different to waiting hopefully for someone to come
along who will make you happier or richer or in some
way compensate for what you think are your
inadequacies. We may try to support ourselves in our
beliefs... "*I can't* make the effort to change my life or go to

the hairdresser or buy new clothes. *I can't* find anyone who likes me enough or fancies me." To do this we use words that disempower, or take away our ability to change the present situation. One of these words is 'can't'. Later we will explore the use of these words and use them as an opportunity to make a difference in your life. Now create and write a sentence beginning: *I can't...*

Using the same sentence, substitute the words *"I won't"* for *"I can't"*.

Say these two out loud and notice if the two feel different to you. Do you notice that the first one has a feeling of disempowerment, there is no possibility of achievement? The second is a definite choice and puts you in the driving seat, able to make more choices, knowing what is right for you in the moment.

H. POWER STATEMENTS

The messages we feed ourselves are powerful and often unconscious and affect our confidence in the world. Usually they are full of "I can't... ", "I always... ", "life is... ", "nobody cares... ", "I should... ".

Do you recognise any of the following?

- Every time I pick myself up, someone pulls the rug from under me.
- I never seem to be able to get it together.
- Men don't seem to fancy me.
- I get on very well with the opposite sex.
- Life's a bitch and then you die.
- I always get what I want.
- I am always shy with the opposite sex.
- Men always leave me.
- I just can't hold down a relationship.

Would you like to come up with a few yourself and record them? You will notice that there are both positive and negative statements. Do you find that either way, they are very strong statements, and very effective in keeping you thinking and acting in the way that you describe? All of these statements that you are familiar with are acquired and learned from past experience.

Now you can experiment with changing these powerful statements. If one of the negative statements written above applies to you or if you have written one of your own, re-write the same statement again, but this time change it to a positive.

Example... *"I am always confident with the opposite sex"*, and at the same time imagine yourself talking confidently with and being admired by an imaginary person.

Here is another...
"Life's a beach, then you lie on it... " and then someone, who at first sight you fancy madly, comes along, stops beside you... This leads to a candlelit dinner for two that evening... and a night of passionate love.

You have the power to change anything about yourself and in changing yourself, so the world around you changes too.

I call these power statements 'POWERS' or POW - ERS! as they zap your past beliefs and leave you free to act differently and have fuller and more loving relationships.

Chapter Three

IT IS AS IT IS

It is as it is... We begin with the way things are, or as they appear to be. Everything in this world changes all the time. Your body is miraculously changing. New cells and tissue are being regenerated right now, and apparently with no conscious effort from you. Thousands of different thoughts are travelling through your mind. All kinds of people are coming close to you, affecting you. You are adapting to the way they are and the way you feel about them. Your body is reacting to the joy, to the stress, to sound, to light, to many different influences. Amongst this you seek to find your unique way of being with others and the environment. This is the way it is. This is your story.

You are already well on the way to deciding how you want your life to be, whether you are ready to begin a new partnership and even relate differently to parents, children, friends and colleagues... I invite you to make your life different. We all live ordinary lives whatever we do, whether we work in offices, climb mountains, run the country, are famous, care for others. What is true is that what you have inside you right now is extraordinary. It is time to attract to you only those people who will accept, respect, approve, honour and love you just the way you are.

A. WHERE ARE YOU AT THIS MOMENT?

This extraordinary story begins with you, and this first section of the book is dedicated to discovering where you are at this moment, what you like about yourself, what you would like to be different, what you would like to achieve, how you would like to get there.

If you want to, you can obtain a notepad, which you will naturally want to keep private, and use it to capture any insight you have during the course of this book. It's fun and valuable to look back again afterwards, and see how far you have travelled.

Imagine how you would feel and appear if by the end of this book, you were ready to decide about new relationships. You are confident, free, released, clear and choosing the way you want to be. If being ready for a new relationship or partnership is what you want, see yourself as that person, having completed this book, having had a rewarding and interesting time, clarified what you want to do and enjoying the results. Now either say it out loud or write it, describe what picture you have of yourself. By going to the end first you can more easily know how to get there from where you are. Keep this picture in your mind as a way of staying motivated while you take yourself through the stages of this book.

B. GIVE YOURSELF TIME

There is no hurry. Give yourself permission to spend valuable time on yourself guided by the suggestions in this book. You are worth it. You may think that spending time on yourself is selfish. Messages from childhood flash across the screen of your mind... *"Don't be so selfish"*... *"Make sure everyone else is alright first"*... *"Look after others before you look after yourself"*... Do you know any others?

My philosophy is that the more time you give to yourself in looking after your needs in all ways, then the stronger you are for other people. Find out how you are, rather than how you 'should be'. Don't be 'self-ish'; that's not enough. It is time to be your Real-Self, for until you are committed to your own well-being, the possibility of a relationship is premature. This is a moment to give your wholehearted attention to the good of yourself. The more you do this for you, the more time you will spend with you, and the more you will find of you, and the more of you there will be, and the more you will want to share this great discovery with others. This is a safe way to a true relationship.

C. WHAT ARE YOU THINKING AND FEELING NOW?

What are your thoughts and feelings at this moment about BEING SINGLE? Allow your thoughts to flow easily, without editing or judging them.

You have probably felt many emotions since your last relationship finished and these may have been: *anger - resentment - joy - peace - bitterness - hopelessness - thankfulness - abandonment - release* and many others. It is possible and usual to feel contrary emotions at the same time. You may feel resentful that your partner left you or had an affair, and you may feel thankful that it is all over, because it was not working anyway. Now you can tell

21

yourself that it is fine to have all these feelings and thoughts, although to you they may not feel that good. They are yours and you are going to have them for as long as you want them, and nobody is going to tell you differently. If your friends say, "Come on, you should get out, and pull yourself together, meet new people", you can tell them that feeling unhappy or unsociable is the way you are right now.

You may find it difficult to come up with any particular feelings, and all that you experience is numbness. If this is so, you can assist the process by noticing anything that comes into your head. It is like priming a pump. If you say "I don't feel anything" and "I've stopped thinking about it", guess what it would be like to experience any of the emotions I have mentioned, as a way of reconnecting with your feelings. If you do not feel safe enough to express any emotion at this point, imagine how you *might* feel and write it down and leave it at that. You will find it easier at a later stage in the book.

D. YOUR STORY

What have you experienced in your life so far?

You can now take a look at the many parts of your life that have led up to this moment, checking back for the reasons and motivation which drew you into making certain big decisions in your life. One of these was to embark on a committed relationship with a partner. Can you recall now those thoughts you had before beginning your life together? Take a few moments to allow them to surface. The following are a few of the comments that I have heard. You may want to add more of your own.

"It felt like it would last forever."

22

"I had this premonition as I walked up the aisle. I knew it was wrong."
"I was head over heels in love. I could think of nothing else."
"My mother said, 'He seems like a nice boy. You should marry him.' "
"My life was so unhappy up to this point. Marriage seemed like a way out."
"I was pregnant, we had to get married."
"We seemed to be so perfect for each other, and I was sure there would be no-one else, so it was perfectly natural that we got married."

E. HOPES AND FEARS

Getting married or beginning a long-term partnership, is often a time when the strongest hunches are experienced, and it is also the time when they are pushed away or avoided. The positive possibilities seem so much greater. Recalling these moments now may give you some insights into what was truly happening for you.

1. Remember now your hopes and dreams, whatever you really wanted to happen, the way you expected life to turn out for you.

23

2. Recall that precious moment when you may have felt that the world was opening up for you, when love looked as though it would last forever, and many loved you and admired you, and were happy for you.
3. If you got married remember how you felt on the wedding day.
4. Bring to mind those times of real contentment, of growing and understanding, and deepening love.
5. Remember some of the highlights, the special events, romantic moments, the holidays.

Then move forward when you are ready to the time when your relationship began to be rocky.

1. Recall the first times you were disappointed by your partner's reactions.
2. When did communication begin to break down? What wasn't being said?
3. Was there something you found too hard to forgive?
4. Did parenting interfere with your intimacy as a couple?
5. When did your relationship begin to feel less like an adventure and more like a set of duties?
6. Did you ever notice yourself compromising or settling for less?

Take plenty of time to do all this remembering. Record it in your book if you like. You may have found that writing can help you to clarify your thinking, stimulate your recall and release your feelings. A fun way is to use a tape recorder. Try it! It can be very freeing.

F. IF YOUR PARTNER HAS DIED

Reconnect with some of the range of feelings you experienced with your partner, particularly up to and around the time of their death. What thoughts and feelings remain with you now?

You can sometimes be left with the feeling that in some way, you are to blame. You could have prevented it. It may have been a premonition you had just before the accident, and you said something and it was not strong enough or you weren't sure. You may have asked them to do something for you, and if you had not done so, it would never have happened. It may have been an illness and the feeling is that you did not do enough or that your partner did not have the best medical attention. Are you left with a sense of "If only"? A sudden death can often leave the remaining partner searching for some reality, and blaming themselves can be one way of creating it. The flip side of this is that you may be left with an angry feeling, almost as if they did it to you, and deliberately left you. There seems to be no sense or logic in this. It is just there and needs to be acknowledged.

"I allowed my career as a Theatre Manager to take me away from my husband during the last years of our marriage, before his heart attack. I played at being the loyal wife technically, but in practice found other people's company more rewarding and stimulating. As he died tragically and suddenly, there was no opportunity for us to communicate, forgive and express love. Unable to consider that I might have contributed to his death, I suppressed my guilt and loss and put even more energy into my job to compensate. It wasn't until my beloved dog died some years later that the grief I felt for his passing put me in touch with the deep well of grief that I had denied. The power of my mourning amazed me, and also helped wash away all the self-blame I had been carrying. Up till then, there was no

25

*way I could have lived with a new partner, as I wasn't able
to live with myself and my true feelings. I decided to stop
punishing myself. I accepted the past and gave myself
permission to be happy again with someone else."*
Morag (52)

G. What Happened?

*"My parents, some friends and relations all said what a
wonderful person my future wife was and how 'good for me'
she was. I now realise I spent a great deal of my marriage
expecting her to be good for me, and wondering why she did
not live up to these high expectations. I believe now they were
impossible, and she also was resenting the 'good for' image,
and regretted not being able to live up to it."* Roger (47)

The following is a list of some of the kinds of information
that it will be useful to look at and which may stimulate
some interesting thoughts for you.

- Your parents and/or relations' opinions of your
  partner.
- Your partner's parents' opinion of you.
- Your friends' opinion of your partner.
- Your partner's friends' opinion of you.
- What did you like and love about your partner?
- What did you not like?
- What did you tolerate in the hopes that it would go
  away?
- Did you have any suspicions about your partner
  that were later confirmed, but which you ignored at
  the time?
- What did you like about your partner that changed?
  "You are not the same person that I married."
- Who left whom and why? What do you consider

26

were the reasons for the break-up of your partnership?

H. WHOSE FAULT WAS IT ANYWAY?

Judgement, criticism, guilt, all become mixed up in a big melting pot of emotions. Accusations can fly and each partner digs further into their bunker, popping up only to fire another shot and ducking when the fire is returned. Occasionally a direct hit is scored and one retires to nurse their wounds and returns later to the battles re-energised with a new supply of ammunition, which they thought up in the meantime. It is a great fight and onlookers stand by and wonder at its intensity. After all there is a lot of pent-up unexpressed emotion coming out and it might have taken years to get to this point. It is time it did all come out.

If you have not expressed it before this may be a good, safe moment to do so. If it helps to give yourself permission to have these feelings, even when it may have been a long time ago, then tell yourself out loud:

"It's OK, Sylvia, to feel sad."

You may remember a best-selling book, which sounds similar to what is written below. I have changed the sense a bit.

I'M NOT OK, YOU'RE NOT OK, AND THAT'S OK. If you want to, you can use this as a statement to tell yourself.

Your truth is completely true for you. It is the way you see things at this moment. It does not matter what anyone else considers to be the truth. It is the way you see things.

27

I. You Can Only Move From Where You Are Now

Some of the questions offered to you in this book may seem to you to be too simplistic, such as "Is it all your partner's fault?" The answer may be "Yes... but I suppose I had something to do with it as well." In this case, answer "YES" as bold as you like. YOU DO NOT HAVE TO BE FAIR. Boldness is the way out of any hole you find yourself in. The more clear and concise are your statements to yourself, the clearer will become your vision of what steps you would like to take next.

Ask yourself a lot of questions like:
1. Was it all your partner's fault and why?
2. Was it all your own fault and why?
3. Could the accident have been avoided:
    - if you had intervened?
    - if your partner had not been drunk or drugged or angry?
4. Could more have been done about your partner's illness? Do you think that you contributed in some way, by causing stress at home for instance?

5. Do you feel that men/women can't be trusted and that is why they left you or let you down? Do you feel a little or a lot like this?
6. Do you think that your parents, relations, friends blame you or your partner, even secretly and they are not telling you? Take a moment to reflect on them individually. It may be just an impression or downright obvious.

J. WHO ELSE IS INVOLVED?

How many others are involved in a break-up of a long-term relationship or bereavement? Usually there are many and their reactions are varied. If there are children they are probably the most seriously affected. There are parents, friends, colleagues and priests and friends of the children. The repercussions are often very wide, and can be the reason why couples hang on, even when there appears to be nothing left for them to share.

There are opportunities for children to repair the inevitable damage caused by a separation. They respond more quickly and easily to honesty and straightforwardness. It is surprising to discover that children have a lot more understanding than is expected, and in many ways the release of the separation can come as a relief. It is the parents who are often left with a feeling of guilt or 'letting down', or 'not good enough' or reflecting on failure and what they should have done differently.

1. How are you with your children right now?
2. Would you like to change this? How would you like to be?
3. How is their other parent with them?
4. Would you like this to be different?
5. What kind of relationship do you have with your

parents/your partner's parents and your relations?

6. Choose some of your friends and reflect how it is with them. Have they changed in their attitude towards you?

7. Notice if there are any changes in the way you are with others and the way they are with you. This could be anyone from the bank manager to the barman at your local. Take careful note of what you consider to be positive and negative changes.

K. As A Result Of The Break-up You May Have...

A. Physical Symptoms

You may have experienced or be experiencing some of the following physical symptoms, and if you do you may be wisely getting help from a doctor or a therapist in complementary medicine. *You are not alone.* The body reacts to the shock of change in your life, and many experience some of the symptoms mentioned below. It does not need to last and you may find that bringing up some of the past to look at may help you to alleviate some of these symptoms. You may need more help and advice, but it is good to know that these symptoms can often be traced back to a break-up of a relationship or a bereavement.

Headaches - Tiredness - Insomnia - Broken sleeping patterns - Panic attacks - High blood pressure - Chest pains - The shakes - Numbness - Forgetfulness - Serious illness - Lack of energy - Alcoholism - Overeating, weight increase - Lack of appetite - Back-ache.

"Even though I have quite a stressful job I had never had any problems sleeping. When the cracks started to appear

30

in our marriage, and Lorna decided to leave me, I could not switch off at night like I used to, and I found that I would lie awake for hours and even when I did fall asleep, I would wake up later in the middle of the night in a sweat." Mike (32)

B. Emotional Symptoms

Shock - Anger - Depression - Aggression - Disbelief - Grief - Regret - Defiance - Guilt - Suicidal tendencies - Murderous tendencies - Fear - Self-pity - Apathy - Relief - Expansion -Elation.

"I seemed to lose my grip altogether. I couldn't think straight, couldn't organise my life, and my body would just shake and tremble uncontrollably. My world was falling apart and my body seemed to be shaking with the shock waves. The only way I could cope at all was to drink, which steadied me and for a while things were so bad that I was drinking first thing in the morning in order to face the day." Julie (41)

It is worth remembering as you check off any of the above list that: nothing lasts forever... this too will pass. Life is continually shifting and changing.

L. CHARTING YOUR PROGRESS

There will come a time when you will look back on these moments, and be glad that you were strong enough to come through them.

Be sure to notice any differences in your physical health. It will be useful to know later what progress you have made from this point.

Recognising where you are now, gives you the opportunity to change your life, to choose a different way, not a better one, just a *different* experience.

M. ARE YOU WAVING OR DROWNING?

The ending of a relationship often means that the work for each partner is doubled. There are two houses and half the money. What is your present belief?

1. Are you waving at the world to let them know that you are a survivor, and showing your previous partner that you can manage without them?
2. Are you calling for help?
3. Are you drowning under the welter of responsibilities?
4. Do you regard living on less money as a struggle or a challenge?
5. Do you feel that running a home single-handed increases your sense of achievement or is it a big strain?
6. Do you enjoy assuming responsibility for running your life now or are you feeling a lack of support?
7. Have you acquired any new practical skills that you are proud of or have you neglected things that need attention (the garden, cooking, the car, administration)?

N. HOW LONG WILL IT LAST?

The answer to this question is, *'as long as it takes'*. It is also good to know that nothing does last for ever, and there will always be new beginnings and as there are beginnings, so there will be endings.

Here are some questions to gain more clarity for you. Be sure to answer without judging yourself to be right or wrong or good or bad. There are no right answers, only your truth at this moment.

Ask yourself these questions:

1. Does it seem that the way things are with you will last for ever? - Do you expect that some day your life will change?
2. Do you feel without choice or powerless? - Do you feel powerful and could you change your life if you wanted to and you knew how to do it?
3. Do you want time to be just as you are? Will you, perhaps, try to make changes at a later date? - Are you impatient for change?
4. Do you need time to be sad, to grieve your loss and to gradually let go of the hurt and pain of separation from your previous partner? - Are you ready to let go and move on?
5. Do you think there is a chance you and your partner will want to have a reconciliation, and are you waiting for this? - Have you decided that it is definitely finished?
6. Do you think that you are still in love with your partner? - Has love faded and gone?
7. Do you think that your partner still loves or cares for you? - Is there any feeling left?
8. Do you think that no one can replace your partner?

- Are you open to someone else coming into your life?
9. Are you concerned what your children and/or other people may think of you if you have a new relationship so soon after the separation or bereavement? - Do you think that it is nobody's business but your own?
10. Do you think that your previous partner should 'pay for their sins'? Do you have feelings of revenge? What punishment do you imagine would be suitable? - Whatever your partner did or did not do, is it all over and do you just want to let them go?
11. Are you addicted or strongly attached to feeling unhappy or miserable about your separation and abandonment? Are you still attached to the drama of the event that caused the separation from your partner? Do you want friends or relatives to show that they care by always expressing concern for you? Do you still need their support? - Do you want to be free of all the attention and start a new life, forgetting the past?
12. Is pain or a negative feeling your only 'reliable friend', who will go to bed with you at night and be sure to wake up with you in the morning? - Are you ready to let go of the hurt?
13. Do you have any money worries from which there seems to be no way out? - Are you financially secure?

O. An Imaginary Game

Imagine that your previous partner walks into the room. Create the scene and check how your respond to their sudden arrival... You may find that this is a good indicator of the strength of your feelings, and will give you more insights to work with, more knowledge of parts of you you might like to change.

"If only..." "I can't because..."

This is the last part of 'your story' to check.

You may have bought this book, because the cover had a message for you, and you are feeling in some way stuck inside your castle, wondering how to get out or even if you really want to. Perhaps you are wanting to break out, but at the same time feeling and believing that there are many things that just do not make this possible.

See if any of these statements match:

I can't because...

- I am not attractive enough.
- I do not have enough money.
- I don't have enough time to go out.
- I need a decent place to live in.
- I have to work.
- I always feel tired.

If only...

- My hair was nicer or there was more of it.
- I was eighteen again.
- I did not have so many responsibilities.

There are many more that you may think of. It is good to wheedle these ones out, as they may be preventing you from moving from where you are now.

This section of the book has been the toughest part of the process, so this is a good opportunity to appreciate yourself on having had the courage to look truly at your memories and feelings. As you review this chapter and any notes you have taken, you probably have a fuller sense of how it is for you now, you will have discovered the areas in which you are most sensitive, and perhaps found some patterns in the ways you have reacted to a broken relationship. Whatever you have been thinking about your life you now have an opportunity to move on, at your own pace, into more discovery of yourself and a greater ability to make conscious choices.

Chapter Four

MOVING ON

In the last section, I hope you developed an interesting picture of your life to date. Perhaps if you have read it or listened to it again, you are already feeling like moving on. Knowing where you are helps tremendously in the process of moving towards clear choices.

It is worth noting that in spite of the 'facts' with which you have presented yourself...
NOTHING IS AS IT APPEARS TO BE...
One moment it seems as if everything is set in concrete and the next everything has changed.

A. ADJUST YOUR VIEW

There was a lion, who lived in a cage, in a zoo, in a crowded, noisy city. Life for him was miserable, but he was making the best of a bad job. Every day he would pace up and down his cage, roaring every so often at the crowd, feeling generally bad-tempered, and of course feeling very much like a caged lion! He had even forgotten there was any other life but this, and his only reality was the ten paces he would take from one end of the cage to the other. All day long... 1... 2... 3... 4... 5... 6... 7... 8... 9... 10 and then ten back, turn around and repeat it again. One day a rich entrepreneur came to the zoo and wanted to buy the lion for his safari park in the country. The zoo agreed and the lion was drugged, fell asleep and was transported off to his new home, which was acres of wild land with trees and lakes. Gently the lion was laid in the shade of a great tree, and left to wake up. After a while he opened his eyes, blinked several times, got shakily to his feet, looked around him, gave a little roar at nothing in particular, just out of habit, and started to walk in the direction he was facing... 1... 2... 3... 4... 5... 6... 7... 8... 9... 10 paces he walked, turned and returned ten paces in the opposite direction. This continued for a while until the sun started to go down, and just at the end of one set of ten paces, the rays of the sun caught his eyes and not seeing where he was going he took another pace... He stopped... Something was wrong... Surely this could not have happened... Something felt very wrong... He felt awkward. This cage is ten paces long, he thought to himself, and there are bars all round and the gate is locked... The sun settled down below the horizon and the lion looked around him, expecting to see the bars of the cage, and at first he thought he could see them, but the more he looked the more they seemed to melt before his eyes and he saw for the first time the grass, the trees and the lakes. At first he was afraid and reverted to pacing up and down... But each time... he took one more step.

You too, are often like the lion - you can pace up and down in front of something and still not see all of what is in front of you.

Read the following sentence out loud a few times and then find as many of the letter 'F' as you can:

> FELINES ARE FRIENDLY BECAUSE OF
> THE YEARS OF CARE THEY FREQUENTLY
> RECEIVE FROM LOVING OWNERS OF PETS.

How many did you see? To most people there are four. Did you see any more? There are seven. Can you see them? If you still cannot see them, count the number of OFs. The reason for this phenomenon is simple. When you read the word 'OF', it is actually pronounced 'OV' and the brain does not register that it's spelt OF. I hope that this little bit of fun has jogged your thinking a bit; reminded you that your perception can be limited by what you think you see.

B. Do You Want To Move On?

Take one pace, one step at a time, carefully and easily, not seeking to achieve some point at which you may judge yourself to be ready, just seeing more of yourself, releasing the bits of you that are not needed anymore.

A sculptor was asked, when he had finished carving an elephant out of a great block of wood, how he had achieved such a fine work of art. He replied, "I carved away everything that was not elephant."

You will know when 'YOU ARE READY'.

C. Holding Two Opposite Thoughts At The Same Time

... and not going crazy.

I have found that 'being ready' is not trying to be perfect. The elephant was already there, it just needed some time, patience, effort and skill to reveal what was already there and as with all works of art, everyone has different tastes. Who really wants to be the most popular face in the world, and look like the Mona Lisa?

We now look more clearly at your reasons for *'NOT being ready'* for a new relationship, and then your reasons for *'being ready'*. As you read this, imagine that you are going to put all the information on not being ready in one box and hold it in one hand and all the information on being ready in another box and hold it in the other hand.

Check through these and see if any apply to you:

D. I Am Not Ready For A New Relationship Because...

- I was too hurt by the last one.
- I'm too angry.
- I'm not good enough.
- First I need to rebuild my life.
- There is not enough space in my life for another person.
- My body isn't right. It's too fat/thin.
- I'm too upset.
- I might hurt someone else.
- I can't get over the last one, I have not let go,
- I cannot forgive.
- Nobody loves me.
- I cannot afford to.
- I screwed up the last partnership. I don't deserve another.
- I won't take anyone. I'm waiting for the right person to show up.
- I'm too busy.
- I don't like being touched.
- I have too little self-esteem.
- I have no confidence.
- I don't know how to relate in that way to the opposite sex. I was married for too long.
- How will I know if it's right for me? I may make the same mistake again. Have you noticed how many people end up with a new partner with the same problems as the last one?
- I'm frightened of women/men.
- I've forgotten how to communicate.
- I don't fancy any of the men/women that I know or meet.

41

- I am afraid.
- I couldn't enjoy being with someone, because of what happened in the past.
- I am not well.
- I just don't feel like it.
- I am not very interesting.
- I am not very nice.
- I can't change, this is the way I am.
- I'd only mess it up again. I always fail.
- I'm trying but it doesn't work. I just feel worse.
- I've got no willpower or self-discipline, no get-up-and-go.
- Who'd love me?
- I'm too critical.
- I don't trust anyone, especially after what happened.
- I like my independence. I'm afraid of losing it.
- If I imagine myself in a new partnership I feel panicky.
- I don't want change. I'm too comfortable with my own rhythms and habits.
- I'm devoting my life to my children now.
- My children could not cope with another upheaval.

It could be interesting to look at this list again and see if your reactions are different a second time. Also record for yourself the ones that apply to you and add some more if you like. Whatever you do, read out loud to yourself the ones that do, so that you can hear yourself saying them non-judgementally.

E. I Am Ready For A New Relationship Because...

Before you begin, let yourself have some ideas about the reasons why it would be good to have a new relationship.

It helps to imagine that you ARE ready for this relationship, so that you are in touch with your inner feelings, your Real-Self, putting aside your fears for the moment.

It may help you at this stage to use your imagination to visualise the kind of person that you would like to meet. This is not someone you know, just an imaginary person with all the qualities that you would like in a partner.

As you read this, for just a moment, sit back, let your breath out in a deep sighing - Ahhhhhhhhhh... End with a smile, if it isn't already there. Repeat a few times, let your body relax and feel it totally supported by the chair or bed.

Imagine a box tied up underneath a balloon. It can be whatever size you want... Have a good look at it... its shape, colour, texture. Put into this box all your fears. Close the box and release it and the balloon into the air. Watch it go up into the sky...out of sight. As you bring your gaze down... standing in front of you... is your new relationship. Anything is possible in your imagination. Be sure this is someone you feel good and safe with. Film stars are not usually the way they appear on the screen. Now as you see or sense this person in front of you... consider what good things could happen for you. Spend a few moments. You can imagine doing anything you like with this person... make it as varied as you can. Then let the picture gradually fade. We will be returning. Now make a note of all the things you did or would like to do with this one and how you would feel, and the good things that might happen for you.

I have listed some thoughts to compare with yours:

- I want to change my life completely.
- It does not have to be 'the one', a lifelong relationship. It is someone I can feel free and have fun with.
- My self-esteem and self-worth go up in leaps and bounds.
- I bring back joy and laughter into my life.
- It is good to feel loving again.
- It is good to feel loved.
- I love making love.
- It is nice to go to parties with someone.
- Having someone to talk and listen to beats talking to the wall or the cat.
- I get a different view on life.
- It is nice to share an evening together and go to the theatre or cinema.
- I like candlelit dinners for two, holding hands across the salmon and asparagus.
- I really enjoy intimacy.
- I like having a friend.
- It is good for me and I do feel good.
- I feel like I'm looking after my needs.
- I forget about the past.
- I like to show off my new partner.
- It helps me in my job.
- It is better than Tom Cruise or Michelle Pfeiffer... It is just what the doctor ordered. I feel a million times better.

I am sure that you will have other ones, and you can cherish the intimate details. If you are recording your reflections in your book or on tape, read or play them back to yourself. Notice how you react and the feelings you experience. Now read again your thoughts on 'not being ready' and visualise yourself holding these ideas in one hand and the ideas of 'being ready' in the other hand. You can hold your hands out and imagine the weight evenly balanced between the two.

F. FEELING NOT GOOD ENOUGH

To make it simple, I matched the sentence *'I am not good enough'* against all the statements about 'not being ready', and found that it applied to nearly all of them. See for yourself and also compare it with your own observations. If you do find it so, only observe it at this stage, without judgement... If you feel like blurting out something like... "Yes that's it, it's true, I am not good enough, and that is just the way I am, and it won't change", feel free to do so, and then decide on whether you want to stay in that frame of mind. I find it useful to say to myself, as I observe myself going into this... "How interesting!" It's just an idea I have about myself, it's not the truth. I then deliberately focus my attention on something else.

I ask you also to treat your reasons for 'being ready' in the same way, just detachedly observing them for now, as if they belonged to someone else.

G. PREPARING FOR A NEW RELATIONSHIP

Perhaps as you looked at the front cover of this book you recognised yourself behind the barbed wire, looking out from the window of your heart. Maybe this is your safe place, from which you go about your daily routine, keeping yourself well occupied, so as not to think too much, carrying out your job, buying food, being sociable and then returning to your safe place. You may console yourself with routine, you enjoy your own company and maybe curl up in bed sometimes with a hot drink, a hot water bottle and a book. Sometimes you pick up a Chinese takeaway or mix with the crowd at the pub, your life has regularity, security, concerned friends, but there is something missing, a feeling of loneliness persists. You tackle this by going to the cinema, meeting up with friends, arranging holidays and sometimes this helps, but beneath all this activity there is the longing to share this with a partner. You have imagined someone very patient, loving, appreciative, romantic, good looking... but that's too much to hope for. Perhaps it is better to resign yourself to your single state rather than waste energy on some seemingly impossible ideal.

But other people seem to find happiness, friends remarry and you share their joy, and yet hurt with your own loneliness.

How long can you stand this. Do you want to change it?

When you find yourself in a hole and you can't get out - don't try and dig yourself out - take a while to relax, look around you at what you've got. There's always more. Maybe you hadn't noticed that ladder in the corner.

H. THROW AWAY THE SPADE

I would like you to imagine you are in a deep hole in the ground. You see a spade which you take and hurl up and away. Look around and after a while as your eyes grow accustomed to the dark you see a ladder. Go to it and put one foot and then the other on the first rung.

Close your eyes and imagine this scene for a few moments. It is said that 'the journey of a thousand miles begins with the first step'. You have found the way to the top. Be sure both feet are firm on each rung. At this point it is good to pause and consider what you imagine will be

46

at the top of the ladder when you get there.

First check your fears of the future. No one goes
through life without fear; some do a good job in covering
it up. Some find it easier to let the fear be there,
acknowledge it and proceed anyway. If by now you have
made that decision to climb the ladder - *just do it* - It's
either up or down and you've just thrown away the spade.

There is no right way that you 'should' take. Whatever
you do, as long as it's movement, is taking you
somewhere. You can tell yourself now - *I can always
choose what I want to do and where I want to go.*

I. DON'T LET ANYONE 'SHOULD' ON YOU

From an early age children are taught how to exist
effectively and safely in this world, and how to keep
others happy, not to cause too much trouble and be 'good'
children. The idea is that they should be at least as good
as, if not better than, their parents. This seems like a
reasonable theory on the best way of bringing up children.
They rarely live up to the expectations of parents. In the

fast, busy, somewhat stressful world we live in it is very difficult for parents to spend the time patiently with their children, explaining the consequences of their actions, caring for them when they do it anyway, and helping them gradually to decide for themselves out of their own experiences how they can effectively live their lives. The actuality is that parents who are short of time, somewhat stressed by pressures of life, cut the corners and tell their children "I know best, because I am the adult and I've had more experience than you." "But why?" asks the confused child. "Just do as you are told. You've got to because I say so and I'm your father or mother." There is a sense of finality about this statement. No more questions!

Do you remember these and more commands being given to you as a child? In order to jog your memory can you please write down the following and complete the sentence. Make them messages that you would have heard in childhood. For instance:

"I should clean my room."
"You've got to do your homework."

1. I should...
2. I've got to...
3. I must...
4. I have to...

You can repeat out loud the sentences you have just written, and take a good look at yourself, where your shoulders are, and how you are feeling as you say them. Next, take the sentences you have just written and change them like this, and say them out loud.

"If I want to I can... clean my room."

48

Now notice your body and how it looks and how you feel. Is there a difference? At this point we are only considering what it feels like to change the use of language to put yourself in the driving seat.

The 'SHOULD' statements give others the power.
'I WANT TO' statements take back the power.

J. IF I WANT TO I CAN

Write some more sentences using the same words -
I should - I must - I've got to - This time use a present situation in your life.

Examples:
- I should wait for a decent interval before going out with someone else.
+ I can have a relationship when I want to.

- I should keep the garden just the way it was when Harry was alive but I feel like putting in a swimming pool.
+ If I want to, I can put in a swimming pool.

- I should be very careful with my money now that I am separated.
+ If I feel like having a spree indulging myself I can.

- I should be sensible and act my age.
+ If I want to stay up until 3 a.m. playing loud jazz - I can.

- I should spend Christmas with my family because they are all worried about me.
+ If I want to be on my own I can.

49

K. MOTIVATION FOR CHANGE

"I should write these sentences" is more effectively changed to "If I want to I can write these sentences. If I decide not to do it no one will know, I'll save on energy and I'll probably put the book down and leave it, and I won't find out that way if I'm ready for a new relationship." It's your choice. Stay on this ladder or step down. Remind yourself that you can stop anywhere you want to. Our bodies are our best indicators as to what is effective in our life and what is not. If you feel good, various hormones and endorphines are manufactured and secreted into your system, which aid digestion and the assimilation of nutrients. These in turn build stronger body tissue, create less fat and supply more energy. The result is you achieve more with less effort and with clearer thinking and you are more attractive both mentally and physically. Is this good motivation?

Would you like to pause at this moment and write out some more *'shoulds'* and *'got tos'* and rewrite them with the formula *'if I want to I can'?* In this way you can make clearer already some areas of your life where you are procrastinating or feeling unsure.

Now is a good time to reward yourself. *Breathe in deeply and stretch out your arms in front of you, stretch out your fingers and wrap your arms around yourself - give yourself a great big hug - squeeze as hard as you like. Let yourself know how much you are appreciated! If it feels good do it again!* If you get the odd crack in the shoulders, it's a sign that it is doing you some good.

BREATHE IN   STRETCH OUT   GREAT BIG HUG

There is an implication that if I don't do what *'I should do'* or what *'I ought to do'* then I am very wrong and will remain so until I do it. Better to start from being right with myself and then I can make decisions in my own life with greater clarity and confidence.

Now we will go for one nearer to home. *"I ought to go out and find a new relationship."*

Change that to - *"If I want to I can get out and have a new relationship."* How does that feel with you? Do you think that there is a difference between the two? One that could help you to be a little more sure of yourself? I am

51

not saying that you are 'ready yet', just finding more of you to offer to the world.

L. A Sentimental Journey

Go back now a few years to the time before your partnership began. Do you remember falling in love or being in love or feeling so good about someone that you thought that you wouldn't feel the same way about anyone else? Did you marry this one? Do you remember meeting someone whom your parents and all your friends liked, and they also approved of this one as being very 'suitable'? Did you marry? Do you remember meeting someone just after you left home or even before, and in some way they reminded you of your father or mother and did you marry? Do you remember meeting someone whom you thought was nice and brought out the compassionate, motherly or fatherly side of you - did you marry?

The above are some of the things that happen to us just before we decide to plunge into a more permanent relationship. You may have experienced a combination of the above or something else. Can we take time out now and taking into account the wisdom you have acquired from your experience of being in a long-term relationship, ask yourself, *"Why did I get married or live with... ?"* Ask your *Real-Self* this question by being comfortable, breathing deeply and remembering some moments or scenes from your life up to the time you came together permanently. Record anything that comes into your mind, however trivial. It may be because you liked sex or the way his hair curled at the back of his neck or the way she cooked. Surprise yourself with some spontaneous answers that can come up for you.

If you want to, when you have done this you can

record all that has come up for you and then ask your *Real-Self* this question:

M. WOULD I DO IT AGAIN - WOULD I LIVE WITH THIS PERSON?

If the answer is *Yes* - ask yourself - How would I do it differently, not 'better', just differently? Make a note of this. It will help you.

If the answer is *No* then you can proceed further in discovering the qualities that you do want in a partner. The bad times do not take away the pleasure and the happiness. Would you like to record one or two of the good times that you remember, and for a moment close your eyes and visualise you and your partner in that scene? Spend a few moments, and then thank yourself for creating such joyful, pleasurable and happy moments. There were good times, give them power, love them, so the bad ones fade and you can let go of the pain.

Loving the way you have been creates a loving feeling inside. It is this feeling that gives you the strength and clarity to attract a partner who will love you the way you are.

If you want something, first give it to yourself.

If you had a new partner now, what would you want to give and receive? - Love would be a good start.

Do you also want: *Respect*   *Flexibility*
                    Approval   *Listening*
                    Acceptance   *Sharing*
                    Trust   *Relaxation*
                    Safety   *Freedom*
                    Appreciation   *Warmth*
                    Peace   *Support*

53

Then you can add any other items that come to mind. Take time out now and reflect on these qualities and start practising on yourself.

You can ask yourself:-

> *Do I respect myself?*
> *Do I approve of myself?*
> *Do I accept myself?*
> *Do I trust myself?*
> *Do I feel safe with myself?*

and so on. Each time you ask the question, some thoughts and feelings may be there. Write them down, anything that comes into your mind. There is no need to criticise yourself. If the answer to any of the questions is *No,* approve of yourself for your honesty and respect your *Real-Self* for supporting you. When you have finished you will have a sense of what may be useful for you to look more closely at in your life. I believe that *what you give out you get back* and in the same way - *the way you treat yourself is the way you are treated.*

N. TREAD CAREFULLY

If you like being a doormat and cleaning up after everyone and allowing others to walk all over you then don't be surprised when they do. If you've had enough of being a doormat, throw it away and start saying "No". You will soon notice the difference in the kind of people you attract to you.

Chapter Five

CHANGE

1. I don't want to change... I don't need to... why should I?
2. I am willing to change. There are certain areas of my life which I like and don't want to change, and there are those which I am willing to change.

Consider these two statements. Which one appeals to you? If you choose A:

You may be deciding that all is well in your life, and all that is happening is the way that you want it to be, and nothing needs to change.

If you choose B:

1. List those parts of you that you like and celebrate them. Compliment yourself for your achievements, and for being just the way you are.
2. List the areas of your life that you would be happy to change.
3. Decide what you want to achieve by changing these parts of your life. What is your motivation?

The sculptor begins with a block of wood, and chips away with his hammer and chisel, until the elephant is revealed.

Change is about letting go of the ways you have been. You do not have to be the way your parents, brother, sister, friends, or partners think you 'should' be.

1. Change is discovering patience.
2. Change is finding your wisdom and your Real-Self.

3. Change is making mistakes and learning from them.
4. Change is creating your life the way you want it to be, and not the way it 'should' be.
5. Change is harnessing your own creative energy.
6. Change is deciding the way you want your relationships to be, and keeping this uppermost in your mind, whilst you 'chip' away at the parts of you that do not fit the picture.

A. THE FIVE Ps

The first 'P' is for practise, the second 'P' is for practise, the third 'P' is for practise, the fourth 'P'...

You 'practise' every day with precision and regularity at the way you believe yourself to be.

You can find out what you are practising now. You have already become familiar with the following: give yourself points out of ten, taking the first figure that comes into your mind.

How much do I approve of myself?
How much do I accept myself?
How much do I trust myself?
How much do I feel safe?
How much do I love myself?

You can see now what you have been practising unconsciously and those parts of your life you would like to change.

There may be parts of you that you do not like, and you are 'putting yourself down' or feeling 'not good enough' or believing that you are not 'achieving enough'.

You can decide now if you want to change these old patterns and institute new ones that you do approve of, respect and trust - then practise, practise, practise, practise, practise!

B. Resistance To Change

If change is so simple - why don't I do it, and why isn't it so easy?

The main resistance is *fear.* When a child lies in bed at night with wide eyes peering over the bedclothes at a shadow in the corner of the room, convinced that it is a huge monster coming to devour him, he lies totally still, hardly daring to breathe, afraid that if he moves it will devour him. Eventually, he gathers up enough courage to cry for his mother who comes soon, and turns on the light to show him that it was no monster but his shirt hanging up in the corner of the room.

Fear is often about something that hasn't happened yet, about the future. We create monsters and dare not move from our safe place in case they devour us. Then somebody comes and turns on the light and shows us that there was nothing to be afraid of, it was just a familiar object. The monster was all in our mind. This doesn't mean that we can get rid of fear altogether. There will always be unknown spooks in our lives. The more we know about, the less they will bother us. Now we can discover what prevents us from change, what skeletons are lurking in the cupboard.

C. IF I CHANGE -

I may not be able to cope.
I will feel unsafe.
I will be out of control.
I won't be able to have what I have got - and there is no guarantee it'll get better.
My friends may not like me.
Other may have greater expectations of me and I may not be able to keep it up.
I may fail.
I might lose what I have got.
I won't get the attention I've been used to.

With this fear of change I will produce reasons not to change.

I am not well.
I can't. This is the way I am.
I'm too busy. I haven't got the time.
I'm still waiting for my divorce.
I can't afford it.
Life changed after the divorce - I don't want any more change.

Procrastination is also a strong way of preventing change.

This is an interesting book. I'll do the exercises next week

58

when I'm not so tired, when I feel a bit better. I can't right now because I'm sharing a flat and there is nowhere quiet for me to go.

D. SOCIALISING ISN'T CHANGE

In the same way, you can make your life so busy that there really is very little time to spend on yourself. If your private life is not too good, there is a tendency to concentrate on your public life. Instead of reducing the loneliness this can increase it. Although at first it appears to improve, eventually it accentuates the loneliness.

Time spent with yourself is the most valuable - it is pure gold.

A motive for change might be to improve the quality of the time you already do spend on your own and so to create balance in your life, by valuing both your inner and outer life.

E. LETTING GO OF THE PAST

Nothing you have ever done was a mistake. Nothing you are going to do will be wrong. What you are doing now is exactly what you want to be doing and you are doing it the way you want to be doing it!

This is a bold statement and one with which, to begin with, many find difficulty.

> If only I had not had the affair, my partner and I would still be together.
> If I hadn't been so depressed and tired all the time, my partner would still love me.
> I was wrong, I shouldn't have left my job; everything fell apart after that.

Apparently Britt Ekland, the well-known film star, once said if only her thighs had been better, Peter Sellers would never have left her.

Would you like to create your own 'if only' statements and when you have done them, say them out loud or to yourself and check how they sound and how you are feeling as you say them? Hold this awareness for the moment.

All that we do is preceded by a choice. Sometimes it does seem as if there is *no choice*, just one way, and at the point of choice that is certainly the case. Our will decides in the moment what is the best thing. These choices are not based on careful consideration of everyone concerned. They are always based on the immediate facts presented at that moment and there is a belief in that moment that this is the best for you.

You love your partner, and are away from home, in a hotel. You are chatted up by a good-looking stranger. After spending the evening together you feel flattered and your ego is flying high, you spend the night together. In that moment you figure that your partner won't know, and that provided you take precautions, no one will know, and it will make you feel good about yourself and in the morning you'll leave and go home and all will be well. You might even tell yourself that it will be good for your marriage, as you will be feeling that you are still attractive and this has got to be good for you both. You go home and carry on as normal and indeed you do have more interesting sex with your partner. Comments are made about this and you mutter something about this magazine you read on the plane. DISASTER STRIKES, your one-night stand sends a letter to your office, you bring it home with you and it drops on the floor by mistake, the truth is revealed and your partner leaves.

Yes, it all appears so wrong now you look back, knowing what you know now. At the time you decided it was all right. Are you now going to deny your feelings at the time or accept that your motive was right?

F. LEARNING FROM EXPERIENCE

Now in retrospect if such a situation should happen again you may choose to act differently. You now have different information and more experience.

What's done cannot be undone. Check for yourself the difference between the following statements, and decide which feels better and gives you the best opportunity for change.

I was wrong - I shouldn't have done it and I will try to change and not to act again - CHECK

I was right - I did it. I have learnt and now I choose to do it differently next time. It doesn't have to be better, I just choose to do it differently - CHECK

Edison failed many times before he invented the light bulb. Each time he learned a little more and then one day he was happy with his discovery. Since then others have improved on it.

Once you criticise yourself you are putting yourself down and so you have further to come up.

Every moment your body is working to keep you in optimum health. Give your system what it needs. It is the same stuff that you would like from a partner. Yes - *love, attention, approval, respect and all the rest* - Do others love you the more you criticise them or tell them they are

61

wrong? Does it make them feel any better? If the answers are *NO*, then start one of the 5 Ps! When you have something as important at stake as giving and receiving love, then it's one of the 5 Ps. Think about events in your life that you are criticising yourself for, feeling guilty about, or taking on guilt because others are judging you. Take yourself back to the time they happened, close your eyes and imagine yourself in that scene again. Think of a good reason for acting the way you did, forgetting for the moment the consequences. If you find you have too many feelings of remorse, tell yourself, without needing to believe it, "I was right" - now see if you can find your 'best' reason for acting that way.

Hold onto the past and your life will continue to be a struggle - let go and you are free to create a new and exciting life.

I hope you have experienced for yourself that it is only your judgement, criticism or guilt that keeps you attached to the past. As you cannot change it, it is likely that you will re-create the circumstances of the past in order to change them or even to keep your feelings of guilt and carry the burden of *penance*. Are you carrying guilt or penance? Does it feel like you are carrying a ton weight on your shoulders?

Visualise - Imagine as you read this that you are lifting a weight from your shoulders with your hands, and putting it down. If you feel that someone else has judged you and put it there - hand it back to them. It's not your guilt, it's theirs. If that feels good, see if there is any left on your shoulders and put that down or hand it over and *walk away from it.*

62

If it feels good just do it - and then let yourself know how much you are appreciated for doing it. Can you give yourself an arms out, round the shoulders *hug*!

Your parents may have told you as a child what you *should* do and then often your friends tell you what you *ought to do*. The one who tells you most of all is sitting right there in your chair.

G. YOUR OWN BEST CRITIC

1. Nobody can criticise you as well as you do.

2. Nobody can tell you what you ought to do as well as you can.

3. Nobody will tell you what you 'should' have done as well as you.

4. Nobody can love you and take care of you as well as you can.

As you begin to let go of the past and to change your thoughts and attitudes about what you did and why, you may be experiencing just a little of that relaxed, warm, confident feeling. Do you have a sense that there is more inside you, you are more capable than you and perhaps others have given you credit and respect for?

Do you remember a day or a moment when you felt so good that you felt you could achieve anything - that you loved everyone and everyone loved you? - However short-lived, do you remember feeling like that? *Imagine* you feel like that now. Is it good? Can you do anything you want to? Can you achieve all those things you thought of doing and never did?

After the breakdown of my own marriage, I rebuilt my own life, using the same approaches that I am sharing with you now. I worked to bring MORE LOVE into my life and more people who loved me and I spent more time with myself, getting to know more of me, letting go of judgement, honouring my choices and making more choices, more choices to *feel good* about myself. Every day now, I find more *love* coming into my life. *Why?* I know now that it was already there, waiting. I just *opened the doors* and let it in. The doors were made up of all my past and all my expectations of the future. My brain, like a computer, only had *past information* in it and so it continually told me to ignore all those situations, which I know now, lead to lots more loving and caring.

H. Making Space

All the releasing and the letting go of old patterns and habits, has been to make space for more to come into your life. Does it make logical sense that the more you 'clear out' the more can come in? Do you have a sense of freedom emerging where perhaps before you had a feeling or thought you were trapped? If you are experiencing any changes in this way, you could expand this to the place where you live.

Do you have *reminders* around you of your past relationship? Trinkets, photos, memories, furniture, decorations, colour schemes that you chose together? Some of these may be holding you back, keeping you attached to the past *not* free to be open to new relationships. You may not even notice the effect that they are having on you.

You may find this idea one that makes a difference for you. Take one of these 'memories' or 'reminders' and give or throw it away or sell it, if you can. Start with something very small and of no great significance. See if that's OK with you - wait a while - if there is a point when it's OK again, go for another piece. Of course, if the idea appeals to you and you just hadn't noticed all the stuff you have around you - *go for the lot*. You may find it best to do it slowly or in a way that feels comfortable for you - you may choose to keep them all and stay with the feeling that they create for you. If 'letting go' feels good and appears to give you more energy in your life, then more of it makes a difference - enables you to be more 'attractive'.

Chapter Six

WHO IS IN CHARGE OF YOUR LIFE?

Now I will introduce you to some people in your life who have been there for a long time, who don't go away, and who you may like to talk to right now, if you want to.

I have already introduced you to your *Real-Self* or *Higher-Self*. This one is always calm and wise and looks at your life without judgement or criticism. It is capable of making decisions that do not look promising in the short term but are justified in the long term, often producing far better results than you expected. Can you remember a time when you made decisions like this, which seemed to be contrary to what you wanted to do, but turned out brilliantly? If you don't remember an actual instance, do you have a sense that you have done this before? Remember the feeling that came with it. Imagine that you have a feeling of calmness, that nothing can ruffle your thoughts, they are like a still lake, you are an eagle soaring above everything, borne by the wind, each feather in perfect unison with the others. Your eagle vision is clear and far-sighted. You can see all that is behind you and all that is in front. You can see danger and safety, rich pasture and desert, sunshine and rain. This is how your *Real-Self* is. You can spend a few moments in your imagination experiencing this.

Well this is one part of you, and if you decide that it's worth talking to this one as often as you want to, you will notice for yourself the benefits that come your way. Remember the *Real-Self* will not always be looking for the easiest way, but it will always choose the best way.

A. VICTIM MENTALITY

The easiest way is often full of people telling you how much of a victim you are, how hard done by you are, how others have mistreated you and it's their fault you are in this mess, and don't you do anything until they put it right. Of course you are hurt, and you will remain so until they admit they were wrong! Let me introduce you to another of your personalities. It's called VICTIM. Everything happens to 'Victim'.

Here are some of the things that 'Victim' says:

> *Everybody always lets me down.*
> *I'm always unhappy on my birthday.*
> *If there is an accident to be had, I'll be the one who has it.*
> *Whenever I get up, someone shoots me down.*
> *In relationships, I'm always the one who gets hurt.*

What does your victim say? - give your *'Victim'* a name and a personality and say these things and be aware of how they sound to you. Make friends with this one. There's one in all of us and it needs recognition.

"Jim and I were married for five years. Then he had an affair. The rows we had were horrid, and on two occasions he hit me. He was drinking far too much. When he left I was dazed, relieved the rows had stopped, and slowly I started to believe what my friends said, that I was better off without him. A year or so later I met Robert. It was great at first, but then I started seeing the same behaviour in him as I saw in Jim. He was drinking too much, and coming home late. Then I realised I was falling for the same sort of man."
Elizabeth (35)

It was at this time that she came to see me, and we discovered her childhood messages. Her father had been in an accident and had blamed his unhappiness and drinking on that. Her mother had looked after her father for many years but always told Elizabeth that if only he had not been an invalid they would have had a much better life. In this way her 'victim' consciousness had become firmly set. After some visits, Elizabeth was able to come to terms with her 'victim' self and make a choice not to go looking for men whom she could relate to in that way.

B. SAFEST WAY

Another one is called 'SAFEST WAY'. This is the one who is not interested in spontaneity or adventure, but prefers a totally organised life where nothing is left to chance, and where mostly nothing changes. It is reliable and can be sure never to take chances. In this way it never gets into any trouble or if trouble does come along, there are many defences to keep it away. Usually it decides that the best form of movement is staying still.

> *"How about coming to the dance?" "No, I think I'll just do my washing."*
> *"I've got this friend who would like a blind date with you." "No I couldn't, I've never done that before."*
> *"How about buying some new clothes and changing your image?" "Well I don't know I could afford to and anyway, I feel comfortable in the clothes I've got. They are sort of me."*

Do you recognise this one, would you like to add to this list? Also remember times in your life when you dared and you are so glad that you did.

68

There are many more personalities lurking around inside us and you could name them. Don't forget the 'RIGHTEOUS' one and the 'ANGRY' one and the 'DICTATOR'. One that may be a favourite with Thomas the Tank Engine fans particularly is 'THE FAT CONTROLLER'.

C. YOU ARE THE ONLY ONE WHO THINKS INSIDE YOUR BODY

No one else can affect you the way you do yourself. It is useful to know that at any time any one of these 'personalities' inside you may be on top. It's not the whole 'you', just one aspect of you and you can change the way you are at any moment.

Ms. Safest Way can become Ms. Daring.
Mr. 'He's always good for a laugh' can become
Mr. Strong, Silent, Deep and Meaningful.

If you want to you can, right now, choose one of your personalities, and then call in its opposite number and act it out. It helps to have a conversation with both of them.

"Ms. Safest Way, you've got the afternoon off."
"Now Ms. Daring, what shall we do first?..."
"Call that good-looking person I met on the train."

You don't even have to make something happen. Just by having an image of this new personality in your mind, the looks, the walk, the talk, you will find that adventure comes your way and for as long as you choose you ARE that personality.

69

D. Most Of Life Can Be Fun

Some of the greatest laughs I have had were with the
terminally ill. There's no self-consciousness and pride and
hoping that 'some day my prince will come' left. When
you think you haven't got much time, and you decide to
live your life to the fullest, you will go into every place
you can until you find a suitable 'prince'. Then you won't
faint or wait for him to find the silk handkerchief that you
inadvertently dropped. NO - you'll go right up to him, tell
him you fancy him madly, give his white charger a bale of
hay and grab him. If his armour takes too long to get off,
you make sure you have an oxy-acetylene cutter with you.

Do you hear the message? If you see someone you fancy,
go and talk to them. All you've got to lose is a bit of pride.
If you don't, they might not tell you they fancy you, then
you will have gained neither pride, self-esteem nor
experience. This deserves at least one of the 5 Ps!

An eminent economist, Keynes, was asked:

"What would you do if you could live your life again?"

He replied, *"I'd drink more champagne."*

This time in your life is a great opportunity. It will never happen again like this.

Carpe diem - Seize the day - Do it now.

There is someone out there *waiting for you.* They are waiting for you to be 'ready'. Drink some more champagne, take courage, you will be amazed how *wildly* attractive they find you. *Do you want the best this time?* Then BE the best. There is so much more of you. We can explore some more now.

E. I DON'T FEEL SAFE

There is always a time when someone else has 'got it', and you wish you had, but you haven't, and you might even lurk close to them in the hope that some of it might wear off on you. *When you walk into a room full of people and you are feeling scared or nervous,* be sure that everyone in that room has had the same feeling at some point. Do you want to stay feeling scared and nervous? They have all got through this fear. You can too.

"Well they are used to it, and I'm not, and they don't have a family like mine."

Being safe is something that takes a bit of getting used to, particularly if you have been brought up in a place that wasn't safe or didn't feel that way. There is only one safe place and that is inside you, and if you are not feeling safe then nothing else outside feels at all safe.

F. Create A Safe Place

Have you noticed yourself when you have been daydreaming? You either have your eyes closed or open and you can see in your mind's eye scenes of various kinds. You might be having an imaginary conversation with someone. It may be a scene that has already happened or one that you wish had happened instead. You may be acting out a future scene which you are afraid will happen, or a scene where something that you want happens exactly the way you want it. This latter daydream usually ends with a sigh and an 'if only'. This is called daydreaming, because you seem to drift off into a semi-conscious trance, and it has a dreamlike quality. Like all dreams, if it is a good one you 'wake up' afterwards feeling good and happy. If it is a bad one you do your best to forget it, but are often left with a sense of foreboding. We can use this ability your mind has for wakeful dreaming to create the feelings and thoughts that you would like to have. I often find that if I have a really good dream, like a 'flying dream' during the night, I feel good and relaxed and positive for the rest of the day.

Here is a short dream for you.

You can do this with your eyes closed or open, whichever is easiest for you.

1. Make sure you are sitting comfortably or lying down.
2. Imagine you get up from your chair.
3. Go out of the room, out of the building, opening and closing doors where you need to.
4. Walk down a road until you come to a path (note whether this is on the left or the right).
5. This path leads to a walled garden, with a high wall and a locked door or gate (see how the door is made).
6. The key is in your pocket - open the door or gate.
7. Go in and close the door or gate behind you.
8. When you are in, roam around. Imagine what it is like inside. Flowers, trees, fountains... You can make it as big or as small as you like.
9. Find one particular place in this garden that you like best and stay there for a few moments, just as you please, feeling warm sunshine on your body and maybe the scent of flowers or just the sheer brilliant design of the place.
10. When you feel like it, get up from that place and return from the garden, opening and closing the door or gate behind you and locking it (reminding yourself that you can come here again).
11. Return along the path back to the road and the building and the room and the place where you are sitting or lying.

These instructions can seem complicated. You may like to write down the general theme, before you do it.

You - get up - leave the building - road - path - wall - door - key - garden - special place - scene - return.

The point of this experience is to create the awareness in you that you can feel safe, relaxed and expanded by your own choice and you are not dependent on others to create the conditions that make you feel good. If you have found it difficult to visualise the exercise that I have suggested, you will remember that at the beginning of the book, I asked you to describe your home or building. You can start by doing this and then follow the road and the path and the rest.

If It Feels Good... Do It!

This is a 'safe place' and the more that you use this visualisation, the more you will be re-educating your mind and body into feeling relaxed, confident and safe enough to be daring when new possibilities are presented to you, especially situations where you would normally be unsure or lacking in confidence.

In all situations of feeling afraid or unsure it is always your mind that creates an expected outcome before it has happened.

"I'm afraid to talk to this person in case they are not interested and I am rejected."
"I'm afraid to tell you how I feel in case you do not like me."

Create some of your own, beginning with:

"I'm afraid..."

Check how you are inside yourself as you say them. Now change them from "I'm afraid" to "It's safe" and leave off the explanation at the end.

74

"It's safe to talk to this person."
"It's safe to tell you how I feel."

Check how you are. Even if you believe that you are not safe, the idea is to change that belief, to feel sure enough inside you to get through your fear, to break the habit and find another piece of you. If you want you can first practise this by saying it alone. It becomes very effective when you do it *in front of the mirror*.

Then make it a 'live' situation, being aware of moments when you feel fear or uncertainty and saying to yourself "I am safe" or "It is safe" and repeating it several times until you feel that *strength* inside which tells you that it is 'safe' to proceed.

This process can also be used in the following situation.

Do you find that you are attracted to certain kinds of people, who have certain characteristics, in the shape of their face, the way they sit or stand, the way they walk? Have you noticed that there are also many more, whom you might like to get to know, but dismiss them because there is a little message inside you that says "There's no way that person would be interested in me." You are turning down a huge number of the population of this world.

G. FAMILY CONNECTIONS

Attraction between two people is often based on hidden or even obvious connections with parents, or brothers and sisters. You may have noticed by now that your partner showed many similiarities with one of more of your family. This kind of relationship will be good to begin with but will, eventually, bring up for you much of the 'stuff' that you haven't dealt with concerning your parents. Unless

you are able to 'see' this and make allowances for it,
it can eventually lead to resentment and rejection.

This may be the time for you to *let go* of all that
and allow the possibility of a completely new and free
relationship to come into your life. You can practise this
by looking at anyone you meet and as you look at their
face, first note how you are feeling or what you are
thinking, then say "I am safe" and see how it changes.
This is a very powerful exercise and you will find that the
more you do it, the more confident you become. You will
find ways of relating to many different people and this will
strengthen your ability to choose, and widen your options.
It is useful to improve relationships with either sex, so do
it with both.

5 Ps - If It Feels Good... Do It!

Now is a good moment for a personal check to pause
and reflect.

Make a note of what is happening inside you and in
your life. Are there any changes, however small?

This way of giving your mind something positive to use is a tool that can prove useful in your life. Remember:

If I want to I can.
I am safe.
I want the best - the best for me now.
Everthing that I do is right in this moment.

H. MORE POWER STATEMENTS

These *'power statements'* or affirmations can be used both to create the situations that you would like and to quieten the chatter in your mind. Before you do anything or speak to anyone, your brain often goes through a whole maze of possibilities, avoidances, fears, manipulations and various acrobatics.

On the one hand I could... then on the other hand I... but on the other hand... *you run out* of hands fast and often either blurt out something you wish you hadn't said or which really doesn't represent your opinion or you may capitulate and say something safe to keep everyone happy. The result is *confusion* which suits nobody.

Use these power statements to quieten the chatter and

still your mind. The clarity that comes from it will give you the ability to achieve so much more in your life. You can easily and safely go beyond your self-imposed limits.

If you want to, you can create your own *power statements* as well as the ones I have suggested. The way to do this is to consider what your weak points are. These are the places where we have most protection. They are the vulnerable parts that will give you that little lurch in the stomach when someone is getting a bit close.

You will notice that each power statement is the opposite to what you believe at that moment. If you say to yourself "I am safe" you are saying it because at that moment you do not feel safe and you would like to feel different in order to be more effective with this person, to enjoy a more intimate, friendly conversation. Feeling unsafe creates the need for protection, and this 'need' builds walls and it is not possible to see or touch through a wall. *You are in control* and your lack of fear in approaching a relationship is the main factor that will help you to decide with whom you want to be.

Our fears are often about:

Rejection - Being taken over - Not being good enough - Repeating old patterns.

Feeling safe enables you and gives you the power to walk straight past these and experience a true relationship with another. This is a relationship between *your* Real-Self and theirs.

I. NOTHING IS EITHER GOOD OR BAD

You will have seen that how you think governs how much happiness you can have in your life and how far and how fast you go in relationships. You may have found that it is fun to change from the way you *always* are with others. There are many factors that will keep you even from doing these simple but powerful exercises. Your brain is constantly 'in action' and if you do not give it some simple messages, 'brain food', to digest, it will dig up the past and 'chew' on that. This is what happens when, for no apparent reason, you find yourself thinking negative or depressing thoughts about your ex-partner. These thoughts can be:

1. I'm still angry with her.
2. There are so many things he should have done and he didn't.
3. I put all the loving in and she didn't.
4. I made all the effort.
5. I can't forgive him for what he did.
6. I still want her back.
7. If only he hadn't died we could have done lots of things together.
8. I can't help thinking about her.
9. I keep thinking these thoughts of revenge, because I feel like punishing him.

We will naturally be having these thoughts, and they are to be acknowledged and accepted. The only consideration is:

Do I feel better after having these thoughts?
How long do I want to go on thinking them?
Are these thoughts useful or constructive?
How do I feel about letting go of these thoughts of the past?

The ideal for you could be:

1. I think it's useful to have these thoughts rather than suppressing them.
2. I don't want to keep thinking like this, so I would like

them gradually to go away.

3. I would like to have happy, more positive thoughts, maybe about a new partner.
4. I would like to be free.

Your mind has the power to think positively or negatively, whichever you choose. You are the one who thinks inside your mind, and you are the one who can decide what thoughts you think and for how long. It is possible to become addicted to certain thoughts, which in the beginning give some satisfaction, but then become really established causing distress and depression. They can seem unstoppable, dominating all other thoughts. These can be particularly vocal and destructive in the early mornings.

"Every morning I'd wake up at 4 a.m., in a sweat, with these panic thoughts going through my head reminding me how hopeless everything was, how broke and lonely I was and how there seemed no way out. I could neither sleep nor switch off these thoughts. The result was that by the time I got up I was already feeling defeated." Lisa (38)

Perhaps you have experienced this or some of the following:

Panic attack - Fear of the future.
Angry and resentful thoughts.
Feelings of hopelessness.
Loneliness.

The only thing you have absolute control over is your current thought.

I have found the following technique an extremely useful one:

1. Be aware of the thoughts crowding in and how desperate you feel about them.
2. Say out loud in a commanding voice - STOP.
3. Immediately after saying STOP, repeat a POWER STATEMENT. This changes your mood and frame of mind.

J. THE POWER TO MOVE AND TO CHOOSE IS ALWAYS WITH YOU

If you choose to you can always:

1. Be in control of your life.
2. Think your own thoughts.
3. Be in a position of choice.
4. Have your own power which cannot be taken away from you. You cannot even give it away. You can only cover it up and blame others for taking it.
5. Have happy, meaningful, satisfying relationships.
6. Have freedom of thought - you can always think your

own thoughts even though you feel entrapped or imprisoned.

7. Always ask for help from others and expect that it will be given, according to the capabilities of the one you ask.
8. Choose wisely.

K. What Is Your View Of Romantic Love?

1. Is it the same now as it was when you first discovered it, or have you changed your ideas?
2. Are your expectations more or less?
3. If you have experienced the moment of 'falling in love' - are you waiting for the same feeling to happen again before you will know that this is the 'right person' for you?

How about creating in your mind some scene from your earlier life when you were 'in love'?

Remember the place, how you were dressed, what the weather was like, how your partner was dressed. What were you talking about? Were you calm and relaxed, or excited? Did you feel you could achieve anything?

Re-create the scene as completely as you can; remember the smells. Imagine you can reach out and touch anything that is around you - *Make it as real as you like* - this scene may not necessarily include your ex-partner, it may be someone else. *Whoever* it is, it is the one with whom you felt *completely loving*.

Relax into this sensation - *Let* the feeling drift through you, up and down your spine.

Place your index finger on the centre of your chest, allow this 'in love' sensation to go deep into your heart.

This feeling of being 'in love' happens only a few times, and yet you have just re-created it. If you have never experienced such a depth of feeling you can also imagine it.

If it feels good... do it!

This experience of being 'in love' can give us a clue to the essence of Romantic Love.

It depends upon another person, and it depends upon:

How much love you are prepared to give and how much love you are prepared to accept.

The amount of love you are prepared to give or receive appears to depend upon the person involved. This may be your mother, father, brother, sister, friend, partner, lover. If you still love your ex-partner, although you are not together, you may feel inhibited in considering loving another.

It is good to love the partner you had, but there is always room for another.

Each person has an infinate capacity for giving and receiving love.

L. Being Safe

In the "I am safe" exercise you were also practising feeling 'safe enough' and 'good enough' to express more love, by both giving and receiving. Being 'in love' depends on your willingness to express love, without limiting it. As you LET GO of your fears, so you experience a more loving feeling. This feeling has the power to break down barriers, in the office, at home - *anywhere*. If you are afraid of getting hurt you will know who or what to avoid for the moment; you will find your weak points, and decide to strengthen them. Did you notice there was a difference in the amount of love you expressed, and did this love take on various different aspects that make up the 'loving feeling'?

Respect - approval - acceptance - passion - support - trust - safety - attraction.

When you get that magic moment, that 'flick of the switch', the 'click', it's as if three oranges have come up on the fruit machine - enough of all the above aspects have come together - and you decide that this is the maximum, I'll stick here. I won't get any more than this or better than this. This is the time for that magic moment. This moment can also slip away if the two people do not then decide to go for the 'jackpot'. They can decide to seek more of these aspects of love 'inside themselves'. They learn to respect, approve, accept, feel passionately and support themselves and then share these discoveries with their partner.
All or some of these can be your *Power Statements*:

I respect myself just the way I am.
I approve of myself just the way I am.
I accept myself just the way I am.
I support myself just the way I am.
I am safe just the way I am.
I am attractive just the way I am.
I trust myself just the way I am.

You can even, if you want to, express your joy about yourself and your dedication to knowing more of you.

I am passionate about myself just the way I am.

84

All of these *enable* you to know yourself better, and with the new-found knowledge, offer more to the world - and receive more in return.

There are no limits to this 'jackpot':

More acceptance of yourself brings more acceptance from others.
More approval and respect brings equal returns.
More 'passion' about yourself brings more passion from others.

CAN I HANDLE THIS MUCH?
You may not have done before, twenty years ago or twenty minutes ago - *Now you can if you want to.*

Chapter Seven

SEXUALITY

Below are a few of the comments that have been told to
me about experiences of making love in a partnership -
what are your own?

You will have noticed how much or how little sexuality
has been important to you in a relationship. Each one of
us has different experiences. You may find it helpful to
know clearly what it was like for you and if you want it
differently in a new relationship. If you have had sexual
relationships since your partnership finished - how was
that for you? Was it what you wanted?

Check for yourself what were your experiences with
your ex-partner and anyone else since. Use your own
words to describe how it was for you:

I enjoyed making love with my ex-partner, we had great fun. I'm hurt they are now with another, and probably doing the same things we did.

I didn't enjoy sex for a long time with my ex-partner. Now I think I would like to enjoy it with someone new. I want to find ways of loving, being loved, making love, which are fully satisfying.

My ex-partner used to want a lot of sex - I couldn't keep it up - but I felt I ought to - this didn't help our relationship. I don't want that again.

I had to do a lot of strange things to satisfy my ex-partner. It was sometimes really weird. I like having fantasies and all that, but not weird!

My ex-partner was the 'get your leg over - do it and fall asleep' type. If I had a new partner I would want a sensitive, loving, caring approach with both of us telling the other loving things. Letting each other know what feels good, and spending time afterwards, holding each other.

My partner didn't seem to enjoy sex as much as I did.

Was it:

satisfactory	*nothing special*
perfect	*weird*
awful	*disastrous*
not bad	*OK but got boring*
did my duty	*wild*

Do you think you or your partner was the one who wanted sex the most?

Who was the one who usually began 'making love'?

Did making love with your partner improve with time?

Did you get bored after a while and want to experience new ways of making love, but your partner wasn't willing to co-operate, so you went elsewhere?

87

Does concern of judgement about your ex-partner's new sexuality, with a new partner, colour your own sexuality or feelings?
Since your partnership ended, you may have had one or more sexual relationships. Have they been with someone who was already married? Did it have to be clandestine? Was it exciting because it was 'forbidden fruit'?

In the sexual act, all kinds of emotions and feelings are expressed, some of these are:

Compassion - anger - joy - need - insecurity - aggression - fear - power (active and passive) - warmth - feeling towards parents, brothers, sisters - fantasies - tenderness - sensitivity - guilt - pain - love.

The acceptance that some or all of these may be happening during the sexual act, allows more freedom and awareness to help understand feelings and inhibitions and also to know how your partner may be experiencing you. We 'make' love, which means that for those moments, all these conscious and unconscious feelings can be experienced and come together in an amazing loving way. No wonder it is a powerful experience.
More acceptance = more experience.

There are many ways that thoughts and experiences arise after a long-term partnership has ended - and you may find it useful to check with yourself how these are with you. Here are a few examples that I have heard over the years.
- *I was settling for sex without love.*
- *I decided the best and safest way was to be celibate.*
- *It seemed that a woman without a partner was considered 'easy game'. Even old friends seemed to*

take the attitude "She should be grateful for a bit of sex."

- *I tended to rush into sex just to assure myself.*
- *My body belonged to my partner. It's strange now, feeling it's mine.*
- *I tried to prove how macho I was by having lots of sexual relationships. The younger the better.*
- *I could very easily 'turn off'. I just didn't let myself think about it. I got married early - I think I went mad making up for all the 'good times' I missed when I was young.*
- *I was numb anyway - I didn't feel much. I don't know why I had all those affairs. I think I wanted to hurt myself or get back at someone. I was hoping that one of them would fall in love with me, so that I could then leave, and in some way get my own back.*
- *I was wounded by the sexual betrayal of my partner, so it felt like having sex was a healing of my wound.*
- *Every time I made love, I imagined my ex-partner was there instead of the one I was with.*
- *I'm afraid of getting pregnant - and I don't want a baby. I've done all that.*
- *I'll have to face all my fears of getting an infection, or worse still, AIDS. I never thought I would have to think about it. I don't feel safe.*
- *I have found that since my partnership ended I have a much more liberated attitude towards sex. I seem to have let go of old inhibitions.*

A. YOU DON'T HAVE TO BE PERFECT TO HAVE A NEW RELATIONSHIP

Every day you are likely to be bombarded by advertisements, comments, glances that seem to suggest something about your body not being good enough. Do you now look more intensely and critically at yourself in the mirror? More lines - less hair - more tummy - less shape - more sags - less sparkle.

Do you imagine someone else looking at you, and thinking the same thoughts?

Are you:

1. Following a weight reducing plan?
2. Using special cosmetics - line reducers?
3. 'Body building'?
4. Having face-lifts - cosmetic surgery?
5. Buying clothes to disguise your real shape?

All of these things can boost your confidence, and may help you to take the first step.

The most important step you can take is to accept yourself just the way you are.
If you want someone to love your body, start giving it some love yourself.

If you felt your body belonged to your ex-partner, claim it back. *Look in the mirror* - tell yourself *"This is my body, and it's the best I've got."*

Stand naked in front of your mirror - a full-length one is best - *imagine* a new partner is standing next to you and *loves* everything about you.

Imagine you are your new partner, and you have something loving and good to say about all the parts of your body - the parts you like and yes, the baggy, saggy and floppy bits. *No criticism*, only find something good to say. *Then see how it feels.* You will feel more relaxed about yourself and then, only then is the time for deciding to take more exercise or make changes. *You are you* inside there and outer changes are not the basis for a long-term loving relationship.

"After my split up I gradually started to come to terms with myself - but the last thing I could really feel comfortable and good about was my body. I still felt twenty inside - and found it hard to accept how much my body had changed. I began to work on the idea of appreciating my shape, my skin, my naked body. This was an important process for me because my ex-partner had been critical and I had begun to disown my body. This really helped too when I got together with my new lover because I could be freer and more expressive in our lovemaking and his tenderness and appreciation of me seemed to confirm how much more relaxed I was in my own body." Amanda (53)

A future partner may well have bags, floppies and a 'pot-belly' too. *Share them* - it can be fun, and free you to enjoy sex with fewer inhibitions.

You don't have to *please* your partner in some way - you are now released.

91

Enjoy your own sexuality - celebrate it.
Follow your own physical needs.
If you have fears or phobias - now is the time to release them.
Touch your own body - it's all yours.
If you'd like to have sexual fun with your own body - do it with style. Make it special, as if it were the real thing. Remember the Woody Allen line, "At least you are doing it with someone you love."

B. LOVE YOUR BODY THE WAY IT IS

I love my body the way it is because... No criticism or judgement - make a positive statement, you can always find at least one good thing to say. See if you can find several.

What messages did your parents convey to you about sexuality and the body? Do you have any of these beliefs? Now is the time to say:

I let go of all past messages - I am free.

C. What You Need From A Sexual Relationship

This is a time to be very clear about your sexuality. Ask your *Real-Self* what you do want. You can establish this now.

Whatever you choose is right for you now.
List your needs for a happy and satisfying sex life.
Do they include all aspects of love:

Respect - acceptance - passion - approval - sensivitivy - warmth.

Start by giving yourself more of these. Use the *pow-ers.*

I respect myself just the way I am.
I accept myself just the way I am.
I am passionate about myself just the way I am.
I approve of myself just the way I am.
I am sensitive with myself just the way I am.
I warm to myself just the way I am.

The more you give yourself, the more you will receive from others - *never too much.*

Chapter Eight

IT'S YOUR FUTURE

A. A DAY IN THE LIFE OF - SATURDAY - MARCH

Had a very unsettled night again. I really feel the emptiness of the other half of the bed. Somehow this big bed accentuates my aloneness in it. Dreamt of being at a crossroads and not knowing which way to turn.

That's about it. At least today's Saturday and I don't have to go to work. It's quite a relief not having to put on a bright face. The office crowd had all organised a dinner/ theatre outing for tonight and tried to persuade me to go. They're all either partnered or too young to understand what it's like. I just don't feel up to launching myself on the world again. It's as much as I can do to keep the show on the road. The car's due for its M.O.T. I've got all those legal forms to fill in and the boiler is playing up again. I get so dispirited. There's so much to think of all the time.

I realise now just how much David did with all the admin and the maintenance jobs. But for a woman on her own, trying to earn some money, keep up appearances, give the kids all the attention and support they need at this time - it's all too much. More and more demands on my time and my finances, and the outlook is so black. All I can see ahead of me is more of the same. Slogging it out on my own. No treats. All the things we used to do together - trips, outings, parties, all the special things as well as the simple things, like walks, picnics and a quiet drink somewhere - have all stopped dead. All those so-called friends, I suppose it's not intentional, they're just embarrassed, but I feel as if I've become socially invisible. The phone goes a lot, but it's nearly always for the kids. It's a very lonely feeling - to answer time and again and for it hardly ever to be for me. God! - I sound self-pitying! - but I can't help it, and when I think of David with his new woman - off here there and everywhere, I feel so cheated.

I've brought up the children, I've struggled through the difficult times with him - and now she waltzes in when he's got the status and security I should have shared. It's not good for me to brood like this - but the same thoughts just seem to go round and round in my head. Time is supposed to heal things. How long is it going to take? I just seem to go down and down. I used to enjoy my own company but these days I just feel a wreck - with all the trauma of the separation and all the upheaval, I seem to have aged. I just look so haggard. Even when I make an effort, you can tell that it's not the old me. I so crave some touching, some holding, but no one would give me a second glance at the moment. It's so painful - especially in this lovely spring weather. Everyone seems to be in couples, to be happy to have things to do together, things to look forward to. I feel as though I'm not a full member of the club of life any more. The worst thing is, I never expected my life to turn out like this - it's all some awful mistake - but I have to live with it.

Saturday today - I'll cook something nice for the children's lunch, try to cover up the fact that I've been crying again, buy myself some flowers at the market and get out a video for the evening. I must make an effort, but what's the use? In some ways I just want to crawl into a hole and wait for time to pass.

SATURDAY - JULY

Had such a good deep sleep. I'm now in luxury in the middle of the bed rather than clinging to the edge as I used to. I really enjoy climbing into bed at night. It's my safe haven, and I don't have anyone else to consider. I can sprawl freely, read late, write up my journal, and just appreciate being good to myself.

Last night I dreamt of making my way into a beautiful garden growing rather wild. I tend not to wake with fear these days. I remember how I used to physically shake,

I was in such a state. Now I don't let those old feelings build up. I just tell myself "I am safe". I reassure myself, I remind myself, I write it, I sing it. It's such a simple thing and it has made a complete difference to my life - it changes my whole frame of mind. A lot of tension goes away just with saying those three words "I am safe". Another thing I've been doing is praising myself and appreciating myself out loud. It felt strange at first, but let's face it, no one else is doing it, so I may as well. Instead of avoiding the mirror or complaining at my reflection, I now give myself some 'POW-ERS', look myself in the eye and say "You are doing so well with so much!" "Well done" or "You look lovely today!" "You deserve the best." I really feel so much better. I seem to bloom as I give myself these compliments. In a way it's a laugh - it's an experiment, and it's working. The children say I'm looking much better. I'm certainly feeling much freer and less at the mercy of my old feelings of bitterness and hopelessness. I've actually got a good system going with my admin stuff - I've organised my finances, and feel proud of my new efficiency. I had a huge clear-out, made quite a lot of money at the car boot sale last week, selling a lot of old stuff - much of it perfectly good, but too charged with memories of my life with David. I hesitated over that lovely soft bathrobe we used to share - I had been wearing it regularly and found it consoling somehow, but it inevitably had a lot of him in it, so I decided I could release it with much else.

Now my space, in all senses, is much more streamlined and I've treated myself to a ravishing new negligee with some of the proceeds. It was very extravagant of me - but it has done wonders for my morale and reminded me every time I wear it that I'm worth only the best.

Things are better between David and me too. We

are managing to be more civil and even quite caring sometimes. Now that I'm better able to enjoy my freedom, I am less resentful towards him. I have more emotional energy for my own life as a result. I've been more sociable lately too. Not with the old set; they mostly belong to the old lifestyle I've said goodbye to. I've just been valuing my real, close female friends. Together we seem to experience a lot of understanding, real sharing and tremendous fun. Being with them has really helped me come back to life. Last night Gemma and I went on the spur of the moment to the theatre to see a touring dance company perform. It was a beautiful evening. We both felt our hearts lifted. There was a prize draw to raise funds for the theatre and to my amazement, I won a weekend in Paris for two. Now that the children are with their father most weekends, I am free to take off - so I will!

There's something else I'm planning - a new man. Much as I'm enjoying life now, with a growing sense of vitality and command, I deeply desire to share this new me in a loving relationship. So! A few weeks ago I made a list - a detailed uncompromising list of all that I wanted in a prospective partner. Even making the list released a wonderful sense of possibilities in me - and I've been reaching out in thought for him. I know he's there somewhere and writing out my belief that my ideal, loving relationship is coming to me. This time I want it to be different - I don't want to make the old mistakes. I'm ready to love again. This way I feel I'm really influencing my own life in a positive way. There is so much happiness possible - and I'm claiming some for me. I know that something wonderful is just around the corner, about to happen.

B. YOUR IDEAL RELATIONSHIP

You have now arrived at what can be for you, if you want it to be, the most exciting and rewarding part of all that you have done so far. A way to bring into your world the most perfect partner for *you* - a chance to design your ideal *relationship*. You have read so far about so many ways in which you can let loose more of your true, loving self. Now is the time to *'let loose a lover'* to match.

Imagine being able to place an order for such a person, commissioning someone uniquely compatible with you, someone who fits neatly into your real world like a piece of a jigsaw puzzle. Imagine this piece has always been there. You just had to sort out the rest of the pieces first, and now you are confidently awaiting the moment of discovery of this one. Does it sound like magic? The sheer beauty of this 'create a mate' approach is that it does work as if it were magic, while being very precisely and simply structured, and giving proven and powerful results.

Too often in life, we let things happen to us. Have you found that your career, partnership, marriage happened more by chance than intention? Have you accepted what was available, rather than what you wanted? Usually, more energy and effort go into planning our holidays than into designing our lives. This is your opportunity to settle only for the best, to aspire to your ideal, to empower yourself to work with the simple, natural laws of attraction, and to bring into your life a loving partner. Do you value yourself enough to award yourself first prize? Everything that you and I have explored together in this book has brought us to this point. We have worked on:

Letting go of the past and making space.
Appreciating and accepting ourselves more.
Being in touch with our 'Real Selves' our real wishes

and what is missing in our life.
Healing our hurts and wounds.
Learning to be strong alone.
Feeling safe.
Experimenting with new attitudes and outlooks.
Ways of being more of a lover - loving yourself.

You are now fully equipped for the next step which you can choose if you are 'ready' for a loving relationship.

C. LET-LOOSE-A-LOVER AND CREATE-A-MATE

There are just a few easy steps for you to take. They are intentionally simple and powerful. They do require your active participation and commitment for them to work in the *best* possible way for you.

I have experienced this whole process myself, and the results were immediate and wonderful.

The essence is:

KNOWING WHAT YOU WANT IN A PARTNER

BELIEVING IT TO BE AVAILABLE

FEELING THAT YOU DESERVE IT.

We shall now take a closer look at these stages, and how they work.

D. KNOWING WHAT YOU WANT

This is a prerequisite to getting it. There is a saying: "Be careful what you ask for because you will get it." This is to demonstrate one natural law which is

Energy follows thought.

If you want to create a new way of living, a new *reality*, it all begins inside with our own thoughts. We may have learnt and created a habit of defining what we want negatively.

"What I don't want is... "
rather than a positive approach which would be:
I choose...
I really want...
I would feel very happy with...

Positive affirmative statements are putting you in touch with your own self-worth and they help bring about a positive affirmative reality - it works.

- *"As soon as I began writing down what I wanted in a partner, I felt free and then it happened."*
- *" I thought that I was entitled to all the things I had written down after all I had been through. I became determined to have them in a partner. I was sure that this was what I wanted and this was what I was going to get. Even I was surprised when we met, at how perfectly he fitted my list."*
- *"It happened so easily, once I knew what I wanted. I realised that on the one hand I was looking for someone loving and caring, but I still unconsciously was also looking for an emotionally crippled mate whom I could allow to abuse me. I made the list and of course it didn't include 'abuser' and I didn't get one."*
  Chloe (30)

David's marriage had broken down. He had lost his job. His wife had taken the children with her, and was living quite far away. He was extremely unhappy. Although she had left because he was having an affair, this relationship had also finished. Their marriage had been rocky for some

101

time, so there seemed no going back.

"I made my list of all the ways I wanted my ideal partner to be. I was pleased to note that this person was unlike my wife or even my mother. I felt that was a good start! A few days after I had written this, I was wondering if I knew anyone who remotely resembled my ideal partner. I suddenly thought of Cathy - I had met her at a business meeting and had not thought any more about her and she had not shown any interest in me. We met again several times before anything did happen between us, and then suddenly it did, and we began a very passionate and loving relationship. We had a tremendous amount in common and found that we both had the same ideas about what we wanted from a partnership. Our relationship just got better and better." David (38)

It can be a very enjoyable time, interviewing yourself and discovering what your real desires are - not in vague ways, but very specifically in form and feeling.

E. BELIEVING IT TO BE AVAILABLE

Listing all your desires is important and deciding that although you have no previous experience either for yourself or others, you can do this and believe in it too.

The world is rich in many people of different races, colours and attitudes. There is a great diverse humanity and there are probably many candidates out there who would meet your requirements.

What is certain is that there is someone who is perfect for you right at this moment.

F. FEELING THAT YOU DESERVE IT

You are entitled to have this wonderful loving 'other' in

your life. There has always been someone waiting for you to 'be ready'.

You do not have to earn it or even postpone it. This happiness is available for you now. You have already won the prize - *claim it!*

When it comes to making your list, give yourself time to realise that you have a 'clean sheet of paper'. You are not choosing love in the way that you did with your first time round. Then much of your choosing may have been unconsciously influenced by your family pattern and by your social conditioning, by your security needs and by romantic illusions. This time the other person may not need to be viewed as a prospective parent of your children, as a good 'provider' or as a 'homebuilder'. You do not need to allow any of your old needs or criteria to limit you now.

> *Be prepared for the unfamiliar.*
> *Be open to surprises.*
> *Invite difference into your life.*

As you grow into a freer more *playful* and independent person, you will not want someone who will need you in the old ways. GIVE full value to the new and emerging you and let this be the inspiration for your list.

G. Desirability

We are all transmitters and receivers. We broadcast a signal into the world that we are ready for love again and another signal, a more elaborate one, a call note, to that 'lover out there' telling them that we want them to hear our call, to respond, to become present in our lives, our arms, our dreams. As we are beaming to them, they may be beaming to us.

Expect this. Be in touch with your own desirability as well as your own desiring. This may be the most important piece of designing that you do in your life. Whether you want a new life partner, or an intense love affair or a loving companionship - it will work for you in a very exact way. The more you are able to specify your wishes and fire them up with belief and power, the closer you will be to realising them.

Many couples have proved and gone on to celebrate the amazing success of this approach. You could join them - *get motivated! Programme perfection* for yourself. Start transmitting on your own frequency.

Locate your lover - beam in your dream - dare to pair - fantasise a new flame - They are waiting!

H. THE METHOD - SIX STEPS
STEP ONE
Create the atmosphere.

Imagine how you are going to feel when you have got to

know your partner, when you have experienced intimate times together, how relaxed you are going to feel. Imagine the big smile on your face, like the cat who got the cream. Imagine that you are posting a letter in a competition, knowing for sure that you are going to win a fabulous prize. Let your enthusiasm flow. Be like a runner in a relay race - start moving now.

STEP TWO
Visualise vividly the person you want to attract.

Remember there are no points for doing this 'right'. The way YOU do it is exactly the BEST for you. It is your own personal signal that you are sending out, and you are listening for a similar one back. It can help to picture 'the one' in a setting familiar to you. Experience yourself enjoying their presence, their voice, their smell, their feel. Daydream a little while about being together. Feel relaxed; if a negative thought comes along, say 'hello' to it and let it pass on, replacing it with another positive thought about what you are doing.

Make it good for you.

STEP THREE
Create the feeling, hold the images and *define your perfect partner*, listing in detail the qualities you desire. Write your list spontaneously, and then use the following as a check. It is important NOT to miss any detail.

My ideal partner is someone who is...

Include:

A. age - gender - physical appearance - health - financial

105

*situation - location - personality - status - personal style -
sexuality - who enjoys - who cares about - who is good
at -*

B. *What are their attitudes to:-*

*health, home, holidays, sex, their family, work, animals,
religion, money, the planet, politics, entertainment.*

C. *What will we encourage and develop in each other?*

D. *Make sure you specify 'available now'.*

At the end of your list, write on the same piece of paper:

*This is my truth. I affirm now that this or something
even better is already in my life and is about to
materialise.*

STEP FOUR
Pow-ers! Making Power Statements, to affirm that this or
something better is coming to you now.

Power Statements are an effective tool for creating a
strong belief system.

For this reason, I recommend that you say and write the
following formula every day, in the evening before you go
to bed and in the morning before you get up. It is generally
useful to write out each Power Statement six times. I suggest
you choose two of the following or make up your own,
being careful to ensure that they are totally positive, and
they are stated in the present - NOW.

- *I now attract to me my real loving partner.*
- *I am now creating my ideal loving relationship.*

106

- *I deserve a happy and loving relationship.*
- *My true partnership is so close now and I am really ready.*
- *My living, breathing, loving, real partner is now making his/her way to me. Something wonderful is about to happen.*
- *Life is about to usher in my new lover/partner. I am ready now.*

Continue writing and saying them until your partner arrives.

STEP FIVE

As you make these Power Statements, notice how you are feeling and what you are thinking.

Positive thoughts can be noted, stored and repeated often to keep up the atmosphere. They may be like this:

- *It's definitely time for something good to happen to me.*
- *I'm really feeling what it's like to know that this type of relationship is at last possible.*

- *I feel better.*
- *I feel positive and confident.*

Power Thoughts.

Negative thoughts can be changed into Power Thoughts. Remember that Power Statements are there to help you change your approach to life. *You don't have to believe them,* because when you do believe them, you won't have to say them any more.

Negative: I'm not good enough.
Positive: I'm perfect just as I am.

Negative: I can't have an ideal partner.
Positive: If I want to I can have an ideal partner.

Negative: I'll get hurt or I'll hurt someone.
Positive: I release my need to hurt or be hurt. I am at peace.

The lover in you is positive, confident, loving, caring, motivated, passionate, sharing, desirable.

Let loose your lover - you are safe.

Once you have created your list and made it stronger with regular repetition of your 'Power Statements' there are other ways in which you can develop your awareness of this other person's existence.

You might like to give them an imaginary temporary name and talk to them out loud, for example, when you are driving along in your car or before going to sleep at night. Another idea is to write a letter to this person, exploring your own feelings and thoughts, your hopes, dreams, fears and if you are feeling really bold, compose a letter from them to you, expressing all that you'd want to hear. Some people like to go further and create a little space in their living area which they dedicate to time spent visualising or 'speaking' to their loved one. All these activities serve to give reality to what you are creating and to feed more energy into the connection that is going to bring you together. You also become more practised in the art of communication, which is the greatest ingredient of any partnership.

You can be as imaginative and daring or as simple and direct as you like. What matters is your commitment, motivation and sense of adventure and self-worth.

STEP SIX
In the interval between creating and getting together with your partner, you can release any anxiety about how or where you are going to meet up. *No self-criticism*.

Respond only to positive thoughts. Have fun - enjoy your freedom - drink more champagne - take up the saxophone - start to learn Italian - go scuba diving - swim with a dolphin - eat pizzas - do anything you have always wanted to and still think you can.

It is in the living of your life, having fun and doing what you want, that you are going to meet someone else doing the same thing.

Chapter Nine

TOUCHED BY LOVE

A.   IT HAPPENS

There comes a point now where it is possible to relax
about the how and the when of meeting a new partner.
You have set the wheels in motion. You are 'beaming out'
and affirming with pow-ers that this one is already in your
life, and is about to materialise and you are ready for
your partnership. Now that it is working for you, you can
release all tension and anxiety about 'the search'. Tension
causes you to contract from the fullness of your own life
and this is precisely the moment to expand into greater
appreciation of your existing happiness, doing more,
daring more, treating yourself well and loving your life
as it is. Someone who is already in touch with their
happiness is much more 'attractive' and noticeable than
someone who is 'waiting in the wings' for happiness to
light them up. The compass has been set for you and your
new partner to cross each other's paths - so you can afford
to relax and enjoy yourself now.

Judy (40) had completed her 'Let Loose A Lover - Create A
Mate' list and was enjoying repeating her pow-ers.
*"Saying them and writing them every day inspired me with
new confidence, and I felt that the most important part of
my life was taken care of - I was free to do some daring
things so I took up gliding. I had just seen an old film about
Amy Johnson, the famous woman pilot. My first day at the
gliding club was a rather bleak day and there was a slight
drizzle. I went into the makeshift canteen and this man*

111

started talking to me. He was a keen amateur pilot - there was no flying that day - but we talked and talked and talked - it was him. It was uncanny how he fitted my list so completely. I didn't tell him till later in our relationship about the list, but we had a great laugh about it.

The best part of this story is that Judy took up gliding for *herself* - not as a way of meeting a man, and yet this is how they met. It happens this way, when we are loving ourselves - more love comes along.

B. 20 Ways To Increase The Loving

Before and after you have begun your new relationship, there are ways of feeling more loving and the times when you will be feeling this are when you are in your most relaxed state. You will want to welcome your new lover with as much love as possible, and then ensure that the loving continues. Stress happens when life on the 'outside' is not matching life on the 'inside'. You have an idea or a belief about how you want your life and the people in it and it's not like that. The result is that you tend to become more stressed which makes matters worse. The way to change this is to practise *relaxation* as often as you remember to do so. Here are some suggestions to help you. Each one of these practices can be done as many times as you want. The 'side-effects' are always positive and excellent.

Most of these practices you will prefer to do at home, and as you become more used to them you can find ways of practising them at work, in the bus, train or anywhere.

1. BREATHE OUT TENSION

Put your hands on your stomach. Breathe in deeply through your nose if you can, and push your hand outwards with your stomach. Hold your breath for a few seconds.

Breathe out with a sigh, and if you can without feeling self-conscious, say "Ahhhhh". This, you will find, is a very effective way of releasing any tension, in a moment.

2. SHAKE

Stand up - straight - start shaking your fingers lightly - then your hands - your arms - your shoulders - your head - hips - ankles.

Do this for as long as you like. This frees the body from built-up stiffness that has been created by tension - and as you will experience, leaves you feeling free and loose.

3. SCREAM!

Do you know those strong pent-up feelings of being angry or fed up, that make you just want to scream? Here is a way of releasing them. Sit down on a comfortable chair, put a large soft pillow or cushion on your lap, take a deep breath, hold it against your face and scream as loudly as you can. Feel the scream come deep from the pit of your stomach, not your throat. Do this two or three times.

4. MAKE BEAUTIFUL SOUNDS

Sound is a wonderful healer. You will have experienced this in listening to music that you enjoy, and indeed this is a good way to relax. Another way of using sound is to sing, hum, or just make simple sounds.

Sit or stand - eyes open - breathe in (hands on stomach pushing out), close eyes, breathe out, and hum any sound that feels right - do it several times - hold the sound only for as long as it is comfortable - vary the tone - open your mouth to make shapes around the sounds.

5. BE A BABY

Lie on the floor - imagine what it feels like to be a baby, all arms and legs - move yourself in whatever way feels good - make any noises you want - this is a great practice for bringing out pent-up emotions safely.

6. SQUEEZE OUT THE TENSION

For quick release - choose whether you want to sit, stand or lie down - eyes open - breathe in - clench your fists - your arm muscles, shoulders, neck - screw up your face - close eyes - clench your stomach muscles, buttocks, calf muscles, toes - and release your breath and all your muscles in one big sigh - as loud as you like.

7. DEEP SMILING

Close eyes - imagine that inside your stomach there is a smile - it now moves to the base of your spine - travels up your spine - through the back of your neck and stops at the back of your eyes - feel it there for a few moments - now let it come into your eyes - and slowly spread over your face - just let it happen - then let your eyes come gently open - and if you want to, allow the smile to become laughter.

8. FEEL SAFE

Another way of getting through fear is to repeat as often as you like - "I am safe" before meeting or wanting to open a conversation with someone.

9. GET THROUGH THE FEAR

There will always be fear - give yourself permission to feel it, without trying to suppress it - then do whatever it is that you are afraid of doing - a useful pow-er to say to yourself when feeling nervous is "feel the fear and do it anyway".

10. SHRINK SOMEONE AND PUT THEM IN
YOUR HEART

Is there someone you have loved and you need to let go or would like to love but can't approach? Are you finding this difficult? Open or close your eyes - imagine this person in front of you - see them getting smaller and smaller, until they fit onto the palm of your hand - then becoming even smaller - now imagine you put them into your heart, by placing your hand on your heart - now put all your loving into that place and imagine pouring liquid light into your heart - stay with the feeling for a few moments - then imagine taking this one out of your heart - allowing them to return to their right size - and release them.

11. BE 'IN LOVE'

Remember the most loving moment in your life - visualise the scene - experience the feeling - bring this feeling into the present - imagine it travelling up and down your spine as you breathe in and out.

12. GIVE IT UP

If you have a problem that you can't sort out - say the problem out loud - imagine putting all of it into a basket attached to a balloon - release it into the air - watch it disappear into the sky out of sight.

13. PRACTISE THE POW-ERS

There are several suggestions for pow-ers in this book - you can make up your own as you go along - ensure they are positive and in the present.

Here are a few pow-ers to say regularly. My experience is that it is best not to exceed one thousand times a day!

- I love myself just the way I am.
- I approve of myself just the way I am.
- I accept myself just the way I am.
- I respect myself just the way I am.
- I *am* good enough.
- I have all the energy I need to do all that I need. (Especially say this when you are feeling tired.)
- I deserve to be loved.
- I love to be powerfully loving. I love to be powerfully loved. I love to be powerful.

14. CONTROL YOUR THOUGHTS

Become aware of your thoughts when you can't stop thinking about something or someone. Allow yourself 30 seconds to go on thinking the same thoughts - then say out loud, the louder the better - STOP.

15. CHANGE THE 'SHOULDS'

Notice how often you use 'should' or 'have to'. Change the words to, "if I want to I can... "

16. LOVE YOURSELF

Stand naked in front of your mirror - find something good to say about you and your body - *no criticism.*

17. HUG YOURSELF

Eyes open - stretch out arms in front of you - breathe in - close eyes - wrap your arms around yourself - breathe out - and sigh.

18. IF YOU SEE SOMEONE YOU FANCY - TELL THEM

Tell yourself "I am safe" - shrink them - put them into your heart - go for it.

19. WOULD YOU RATHER BE RIGHT OR
WOULD YOU RATHER BE HAPPY?

Be a good listener - listen unconditionally to what your partner has to say.

20. YOUR REAL-SELF

All these practices will help you to be in touch with your Real-Self - your Real-Self wants only peace, happiness, comfort, and lots of loving - and knows exactly how to achieve all of them.

C. COMMUNICATION
Touched by real love... and more.

You can experience all your dreams of lasting love and intimacy with a partner - there is only one way that will ensure this... *communication*.

When you feel you know your partner well enough, become Mr. or Ms. Daring.

- Start to tell each other your fears.
- Talk about the bits of your body that you think aren't good enough - laugh a lot!

118

- Talk about your hopes and dreams.
- Share your losses - and unspoken griefs.
- Be a patient listener.

Above all keep the communication going. If you don't tell your partner about you - they will make it up!

- Create emergency agreements - How to be with each other.
- Be tolerant - when old patterns and habits show themselves.
- Be fully aware that there is *your truth* and *their truth* and everyone will see things differently. It's just the way you see things and you can accept that they see it differently. (The Fs). You don't have to agree, just accept that they have this truth.
- Look for the same kind of happiness you share with each other, in other people, in other couples, in your relationship with anyone.
- If you have a thought, share it now with your partner There is not an ideal or a better time. If you think it - it means it wants to be shared *now.*
- If you have a 'block' or problem that you cannot shift *give up!* Give it up into the atmosphere - watch it disappear. If you release worrying, you are letting go of any negative pictures you may have of the outcome. Then nature takes a hand. Only when you are relaxed and not nagging at a problem - does it become sorted out.

D. Do All The Things You Didn't Do Before

Touch, cuddle, play together, be creative, talk, run, walk,

cook, imagine, visualise, use *Pow-ers*, contact *Real-Self*.
If some of it feels a bit uncomfortable or unnatural, it's
only because you are not used to it. *The more you do it -
the better it feels*.

You can retain your identity in every way. It is what
you bring to the partnership. Don't be in a hurry to
throw everything together.
Enhance the positive. Look for things in your partner to
praise. Thank them for all their ways which please you.
Be in love - that depends on you and not on your
partner - it can last forever.
There is a special reason why you two have come
together. With your new partner you can say much
more than you ever have because they reflect you
so well. This is a unique moment. You are either about
to let-loose-a-lover, create-a-mate or you have one
already. Cast all cares to the wind - this is the time to
release inhibitions.

YOU <u>ARE</u> READY!